Wartime America

WARTIME AMERICA

The World War II Home Front

John W. Jeffries

The American Ways Series

IVAN R. DEE   _Chicago_

Library of Congress Cataloging-in-Publication Data:
Jeffries, John W., 1942–
    Wartime America : the World War II home front / John W. Jeffries.
       p. cm. — (American ways series)
    Includes bibliographical references and index.
    ISBN 1-56663-118-1. — ISBN 1-56663-119-X (pbk.)
    1. World War, 1939–1945—United States.   I. Title.
II. Series.
D769.J44 1996
940.54'0973—dc20   96-18600

For Martha and Bill

Contents

Preface

AFTER MORE THAN half a century, World War II continues to resonate powerfully in the consciousness of the American people and to shape understandings of modern American history. And well it might, for in addition to its immense global impact and its enormous consequences for the international power and role of the United States, the Second World War left its mark on the American home front and postwar American life. Two perspectives especially have framed analyses of the wartime experience: the idea of World War II as a "watershed," a major turning point in American history; and the identification of World War II as the "Good War" of national unity, virtue, and success. Although widely accepted, these two views of the impact and meaning of the war have also provoked important debate.

With the frameworks of a watershed and the Good War in mind, this book aims within its brief compass to probe the history of wartime America and to assess the domestic impact of the war. I have necessarily omitted much detail, which can be found in readings suggested in the Note on Sources at the end of the book. My purpose is not to provide an exhaustive chronicle of the war years but rather to illuminate the principal features of the home-front experience and to explore the significance of World War II for the American people and their economy, society, and political system.

I have incurred numerous debts in writing this book, debts that I can only partly list and can even less adequately repay. I thank John Braeman and Ivan Dee for inviting me to con-

tribute to the American Ways Series and for their help and pa-
tience on the long path to publication. I have profited enormously from the books and articles written by other scholars
and from discussions and occasional debates over the years
with colleagues and students. John Blum, John Braeman,
Warren Cohen, Roger Daniels, Ivan Dee, Nancy Diamond,
and William Tuttle have read the manuscript and offered
many helpful comments and suggestions. The staff of the
Albin O. Kuhn Library of the University of Maryland Baltimore County has again provided ready assistance, and my
talented colleagues and good friends in the UMBC history department have given help and support in a variety of ways.
Sabbatical leave in the fall term 1995 enabled me to complete
the book. John Morton Blum has provided important advice,
encouragement, and friendship as well as a model of scholarship for more years than either of us might care to remember.
I thank Nancy Diamond for her friendship and counsel and
for her discerning editorial eye. My friends on North Hilltop
Road and in the New Year's group have sustained me and en-
riched my life. I owe most to my family—to my wife, Renate,
essential to this enterprise as to all the others; to our wonderful
children, Martha and Bill, dearer to me than I can say; and to
Scott, a son-in-law to cherish.

J. W. J.

Catonsville, Maryland
June 1996

Wartime America

1

Wartime America: Frameworks and Meanings

WARTIME AMERICANS quickly recognized that World War II was likely a turning point in history. Recalling the day of the Japanese attack on Pearl Harbor, December 7, 1941, the journalist Marquis Childs remembered "all of us saying, 'Nothing will ever be the same again.'" And, he concluded more than three decades later, "it never was the same. It never will be." Americans also soon came to understand that World War II brought not only the defeat of the Axis powers but also unparalleled prosperity, unexpected personal gains, and enormous national power and possibilities. Frankie Cooper, a young woman who moved from rural Kentucky to East St. Louis and to new opportunities during the war, said, "My experiences during World War II changed my whole life. I know it's terrible to say that about a war, but I can't recall anything about it that wasn't good for me."[*]

[*]The United States was at war from the attack on Pearl Harbor and the American declaration of war in early December 1941 until the surrender of Japan in late summer 1945. But World War II began in Europe in September 1939; and over the next two years, war abroad, the erosion of American neutrality, and the developing national defense program had important effects on the nation's economy, society, and politics. In significant ways, then, "wartime America" encompasses the entire period from 1939 to 1945.

These two ideas—that World War II was a fundamental divide, a "watershed," in American history, and that it was the "Good War"—have provided the dominant frameworks for understanding the impact and meaning of World War II. Both echoed resoundingly through the fiftieth anniversary celebrations of the war. But those ideas have also been challenged, by historians who emphasize basic continuities in the era and by those who argue that the notion of the Good War is more fable than fact.

A WATERSHED?

A widespread understanding exists among scholars and the public alike that World War II was a decisive turning point in American history, a "watershed" that in virtually every area of life clearly separated prewar from postwar America. In a special section of the *Washington Post* in the summer of 1995 devoted to "Remembering World War II," Haynes Johnson wrote that "Socially, politically, economically, militarily, culturally, racially, sexually, demographically, even mythologically, World War II was the crucible that forged modern America. It was *the* transforming event that reshaped all who lived through it, and continues to affect those born after it."

With respect to the nation's economy, the watershed interpretation holds that the war produced national prosperity, lifted living standards and expectations, expanded the middle class, strengthened and diversified the economies of the South and West, and made the United States the world's economic giant. Wartime technology (and the government's role in it) produced not only such instruments of war as radar and the atomic bomb but also the computer revolution and the development of new wonder drugs, insecticides, and synthetic materials.

The argument for World War II as a fundamental divide

also involves the nation's political system. Greatly increasing the size, reach, and cost of the federal government, the war enlarged the power of the presidency, ushered in the "Keynesian revolution" in fiscal policy, and changed the liberal agenda. At the same time, paradoxically, congressional conservatives were able to stymie further New Deal reform; big business gained greater economic and political power; and a "military-industrial complex" took shape. A modern "organizational society" dominated by large institutions characterized postwar America as big government, big business, big labor, and big farming all grew in size and influence during the war.

But the idea of World War II as a watershed in national life has come to focus especially on the social consequences of the war. For African Americans and for women, the war challenged old roles and norms and appeared to lay the foundation for the postwar civil rights and women's movements. Helping to integrate white ethnic groups into the society's mainstream, the war also brought important changes for Native Americans and Mexican Americans. Servicemen (and sometimes women) encountered extraordinary new circumstances and experiences, gained vital new training and skills, and profited from the GI Bill. And World War II sped the growth of the Sunbelt states of the South and West, spurred the expansion of metropolitan areas and suburbs, and launched a marriage and baby boom of great proportions and still greater implications. In these and other ways, the war bred new experiences, opportunities, and aspirations and seemed to hasten the democratization and homogenization of American life. Old values and expectations were often challenged, sometimes shattered; new ones began to form.

In all—and the case has only been sketched here—a strong argument exists for World War II as a crucial turning point in American domestic history as well as in the nation's foreign policy and global role. Yet for all the evidence of the war's powerful impact on American life, there is another perspective, one that stresses important continuities in the era and suggests that the watershed interpretation exaggerates or oversimplifies the war's impact.

The analytical and interpretive questions at issue are important, indeed fundamental. They involve the very nature of historical change. Does societal change come suddenly, or slowly—or in some often complex combination of change and continuity? What role does war play in shaping societies and states? What was the impact of World War II on the United States? Thinking back to the war years, Rudolph Spitzer of Kenmore, New York, concluded that "the effect of the war on our town was probably no different than on thousands of similar communities throughout the nation—boom times . . . and then a gradual settling down to normalcy. Apart from that, I cannot see much change." And does comparing postwar with prewar America and attributing changes to the war involve the fallacy of thinking that because one thing follows another it was necessarily caused by it? Reflecting in the mid-1970s on the war's impact, Anna Mae Lindberg said, "I'm definitely a different person now than I was then, but I don't know how much the war had to do with it." Did the great apparent changes of war years happen *because* of the war—or merely *during* the war?

In fact, a strong challenge can be mounted to the watershed interpretation. Many areas and communities in the United States experienced relatively little direct impact of war. Recent analyses even of wartime California, seemingly a major example of the war's transforming impact, point strongly to deep-rooted continuities. Nationally there was little change in the distribution of wealth and power. Political party appeals, voting patterns, and the fundaments of domestic policy remained much as they had been before the war. Cross-national comparative studies suggest how much less World War II affected the United States than it did the other principal combatants and much of the rest of the world. Returning home after overseas assignment, Marquis Childs was struck by how he "felt things were still so normal here, that we hadn't been touched by the war."

Long-term historical perspective suggests that many of the changes associated with the war had long been under way—including new roles for women, altered circumstances and civil rights activism for blacks, the integration of white ethnic groups, the rise of suburbs and the Sunbelt, the emergence of the "organizational society," the growing size and role of the federal government, and the slowing and reorientation of the New Deal. The war may have reinforced or accelerated or redirected such changes, but it did not necessarily produce them.

Nor did World War II complete or consummate many of the changes commonly attributed to it. It took the civil rights movement a decade after 1945 to develop great momentum, the women's movement more than two decades; and both women and African Americans remained at war's end constrained by discrimination and old norms. The baby boom, the mushrooming of the suburbs, the impact of new technologies, and the maturation of the military-industrial complex were also more evident after than during the war. The war may have galvanized such changes, but it did not complete them, and any reckoning of the shaping of modern America must take into account the postwar (and prewar) eras as well as the war years.

Nor, finally, should it be assumed that the war revolutionized American values and norms. One reason for the incompleteness of social and cultural changes often associated with the war was the continuing hold of old values, old ideas, and old patterns of life with respect to race, gender, family and community life, and much else besides. Wartime Americans

tended to visualize the postwar era as a more prosperous version of prewar America; they wanted good times, not hard
times, but most wanted no radical alterations in the fabric of
national life. They wanted changes in personal circumstance
and opportunity, not in broad social patterns and norms.

There is reason then to question the watershed thesis—or,
more precisely, a need carefully to specify the mix of change
and continuity and the role of the war in wartime and postwar
developments. The answers are not easy or obvious, but the
effort is essential if one is to understand the impact of World
War II on American life.

A Good War?

At the 1989 annual meeting of the Organization of American Historians, a panel of scholars was assembled to observe
the fiftieth anniversary of the beginning of World War II and
"to tie their own [wartime] experience to the historiography of
the war years." The historians scarcely mentioned the long-
term consequences of the war or the notion that World War II
was a turning point in American history. Rather, there
emerged from the panelists a wartime picture of Jim Crow
discrimination and segregation for African Americans, of limited opportunities for women, of the incarceration of Japanese
Americans, and of the brutality and callousness of combat. Responding from the audience, the women's historian Gerda
Lerner, who was able to emigrate from Hitler's Europe to the
United States but whose mother died before gaining entry,
talked angrily about the pervasive anti-Semitism that shaped
American policy toward refugees from the Nazi Holocaust.
While Bradford Perkins, an historian of American foreign
policy, suggested that World War II had been a "good war" in
which the burdens of a just cause had been widely shared, the
moderator, Richard Wightman Fox, concluded that the dis-

cussion had revealed a "sad contradiction between American pretensions and American realities" in the war era.

This discussion among historians reflected recent tides in the interpretation of the war years. It revealed for one thing the growing attention to social history and to issues of race, gender, and ethnicity that has increasingly informed the study of American history. It also reflected the sharp challenge emerging among historians to the notion of World War II as the Good War. And the discussion revealed the gap that often exists between scholarly analysis and popular understandings of history, for the observations of these historians were generally at sharp odds with the theme of the Good War that pervaded so many of the fiftieth-anniversary recollections and celebrations of the war.

The identification of World War II as the Good War is essentially a postwar phenomenon, a product to an important degree of nostalgia and selective memory, of movies and the media, and of changing times and lengthening perspectives. Wartime Americans thought the war a necessary war, a just war, ultimately a successful war, but not necessarily a "good" war. Even as they enjoyed wartime prosperity and feared that peace might mean a return to prewar economic stagnation, they longed for the war to be over. When the end came, Americans celebrated victory and embraced the national power, prosperity, and possibilities that accompanied it, but not usually the war itself or even their wartime experiences, satisfying and rewarding though many had found them.

By the early 1950s, however—the era of Korea, McCarthyism, and the "mess in Washington"—World War II was already being remembered as a shining moment of American unity, virtue, and greatness. Not coincidentally, a hero of that war, Dwight D. Eisenhower, was elected president in 1952. By the 1960s and 1970s, with the divisive Vietnam War and the apparent decline of American strength and success at home and abroad, World War II seemed by comparison all the more the Good War of American virtue, common cause, triumph, and unexpected but deserved rewards. The nostalgic and celebratory observations and reminiscences of 1989 to 1995 both reflected and reinforced the notion of the Good War.

The idea of the Good War has several interconnected dimensions. One is that World War II was a just war, fought against Axis evil and aggression in Europe and the Pacific, fought with evident unity and common cause toward the great victories of 1945. Emerging as the preeminent economic, military, and political power on the globe, the United States, in this view, sought neither territorial gains nor a vengeful peace but rather helped to rebuild Europe, construct a democratic Germany and Japan, and keep the peace and protect American interests and principles in the postwar era.

At home, World War II seemed a Good War for bringing not only full employment, unprecedented general prosperity, the explosive postwar growth of the middle class, and rising standards of living but also new opportunities and expectations for women, African Americans, ethnic groups, farmers, and the working class. All this was accomplished without the sort of repressive home-front policies and social sanctions that had violated civil liberties during World War I, and without the bloody costs of the American Civil War or of the other major combatants in the First and Second World Wars.

The war ended with an expansive sense of American achievement and a widespread conviction that American virtue underlay American strength, that American right and American might were intertwined. Laura Briggs, whose Idaho farm family went from poverty to prosperity and whose own horizons and aspirations were enlarged by the war, recalled that "When the war was over we felt really good about ourselves. We had saved the world from an evil that was unspeakable. . . . Life was going to be glorious from now on, because we deserved it. Good times were going to go on and on; everything was going to get better. It was just a wonderful happy ending."

But there have always been qualifications to or dissent from the idea of the Good War. Wartime Americans knew that World War II was not one of unalloyed virtue, or success, or happiness. There was too much self-seeking and expediency, too much social tension and conflict, too much anxiety and frustration, too much heartache and even tragedy. Looking back, men and women who lived through the war have some-times blamed it for disrupting old ways of life, for weakening community bonds, for making government and big business too powerful, and for other unwelcome or troubling change. Some historians, especially on the left, have long provided al-ternatives to the concept of the Good War.

Ironically, the book that helped publicize the notion of the Good War—Studs Terkel's *"The Good War,"* a collection of oral histories published in 1984—in fact carries messages at odds with the apparent meaning of its title. In a note follow-ing his title page, Terkel explained that he used quotation marks around the words "the good war" because, he said, "the adjective 'good' mated to the noun 'war' is so incongruous." But Terkel's book contains much more that challenges and even subverts the idea of the Good War. In the recollections he included can be found evidence for the savage brutality of war and its awful consequences for innocents and civilians, for ways in which the waging of war militated against justice and social reform, and for the view that World War II helped to institutionalize militarism by seeming to show that war was the way to prosperity, progress, and solutions.

Partly prompted by celebratory observations of World War II, a vigorous new literature has emerged that challenges the notion of the Good War. In his influential 1989 book *Wartime*, the literary scholar and World War II combat veteran Paul

Fussell claimed that "For the past fifty years the Allied war has been sanitized and romanticized almost beyond recognition by the sentimental, the loony patriotic, the ignorant, and the bloodthirsty." There had been "so much talk about 'The Good War,' the Justified War, the Necessary War, and the like," he wrote, "that the young and the innocent could get the impression that it was really not such a bad thing after all. It's thus necessary to observe that it was a war and nothing else, and thus stupid and sadistic. . . ."

Fussell sought "to balance the scales." In his fierce and often shocking book, he told of production snarls, inferior equipment, egregious and disastrous blunders, self-seeking and self-promoting leaders, barbarous and terrifying savagery that produced mutilated bodies and psyches, and a lack of any real ideological or principled understanding of the war's purpose among wartime Americans.

Other scholars have systematically challenged the idea of a Good War on the American home front. They stress for one thing the degree to which prejudice and discrimination shaped American conduct of the war—including the removal and incarceration of Japanese Americans on the West Coast, the reign of Jim Crow discrimination and segregation against African Americans, limited and short-lived gains for American women, constricted chances for Hispanics and American Indians, home-front anti-Semitism, and discrimination and infringements of rights for homosexuals, especially in the armed forces. Such patterns not only abridged opportunity and democracy but also hindered the American war effort.

This more critical view of the war years maintains as well that the war tended to help the rich and the powerful more than the poor and the marginal. Big business and big farmers gained additional economic and political power at the expense of small business, labor, and small farmers. There was little or no real redistribution of wealth and economic power, and the income tax reached into the pockets of middle-class and working-class Americans. Even the seemingly incontrovertible fact of wartime prosperity has been challenged. And, say critics, such developments as nuclear fission, new petrochemical products, and DDT produced environmental damage and health perils.

Nor by this account was the home front simply a place of common cause and good times. Families and communities were disrupted, wartime migrants were often disdained and ostracized, racial violence sometimes erupted (most notably in the troubled summer of 1943), and many veterans returned scarred and maimed, sometimes even feared. Shortages, rationing, and restrictions rankled and gave rise to selfishness, favoritism, and a black market.

Finally, so this alternative interpretation runs, the federal government became more coercive and intrusive as it became more powerful. Not only did the government allow and sometimes sanction discrimination against minorities, of which the incarceration of innocent Japanese-American citizens was the most obvious, but it conscripted men and money, censored and shaped news reporting and photography, effectively censored Hollywood, and infringed upon First Amendment rights of free speech. Critics argue that the government wanted its own purposes and messages, not necessarily the realities of the war, portrayed to the American people, and that journalists, academics, and others sometimes violated their professional standards, and both liberals and conservatives their principles, in doing the government's bidding. And the aims of such manipulation and obfuscation were not just victory and unity but also personal, corporate, and political gain.

Several perspectives will help in sorting through these often complicated claims and counterclaims about wartime America. For one thing, the issues are to an important extent ones of balance and focus. One can find both change and continuity in the war years, both successes and shortcomings. Comparative analyses—both chronological and cross-national—are useful. The World War II American home front, for example, was not as repressive or illiberal as the World War I home front, nor did Americans experience the impact of the war or controls over their lives and expression that other World War II belligerents suffered, including the British. Victory and national survival are the overriding concerns of nations at war; other societal values and priorities, sometimes even basic ones, are often secondary, at least for the duration.

Compared with the watershed interpretation, the idea of the Good War turns more on value judgments than on analytical scholarship. However difficult it is to define and measure the type, extent, and rate of change that constitute a "watershed," however hard to come to a general conclusion about the war's impact when it differed from person to person, group to group, area to area, it is harder still to find a moral calculus or consensus on a "good war." Some would argue in any case that historians should seek to analyze, understand, and explain rather than offer moral judgments. In this respect the two dominant frameworks for understanding World War II have quite different dimensions.

In another sense, however, the two frameworks are often mirror images of one another. To a significant extent the view of the war as a domestic watershed suggests that it was a Good War at home: it restored prosperity; it provided new opportunities; it improved the status and prospects of women, African Americans, and the working class; and so on. By contrast, challenges to the idea of the Good War on the home front are often, implicitly at least, also challenges to the notion of the war as a great divide: long-standing prejudice, for example, limited the gains of African Americans, of women, and of other minorities; the great wartime gains went to the already rich and powerful and accentuated inequalities; deep-rooted social divisions persisted.

Finally, to understand wartime America and the impact and nature of World War II requires remembering that history is not just the story of massive, impersonal forces moving societies this way and that. It is also the story of men and women acting in time and circumstance, of the interactions between large forces on the one hand and ideas and individual intent and action on the other. As Bruce D. Porter has put it in his book *War and the Rise of the State*, to say that war causes certain effects "is only a convenient shorthand; what really happens is that state leaders, governments, military officers, armies, and populations . . . cause those effects to occur."

Using the related interpretive frameworks of a watershed and the Good War, this book explores the impact of World War II on the American people and the meanings that wartime Americans, individually and collectively, sought and found in the war. The historians Roger W. Lotchin and Martin Schiesl have observed that there were really "many different home fronts"; certainly there were many different experiences in wartime America, a variety of stories and developments that must be probed to gauge the domestic impact and meaning of World War II.

2

Mobilizing the Economy

WAR, the American intellectual Randolph Bourne noted with grim irony in opposing involvement in World War I, "is the health of the state." Certainly that was the case for wartime America, as the federal government grew during World War II to a size and strength far beyond the New Deal state of the 1930s. The number of federal civilian employees quadrupled, from some 950,000 in 1939 to 3.8 million in 1945. Expenditures soared elevenfold, from not quite $9 billion to over $98 billion in those same years, from about one-tenth to nearly half the Gross National Product. The power of the executive branch expanded enormously as the government controlled production, materials, and labor, rationed goods and set prices, spent and taxed more than it ever had before. After the war, because of the "ratchet" effect, the government did not revert to its prewar dimensions; in 1950, for example, the federal government had almost two million civilian employees—about half the 1945 total but twice that of 1939.

Mobilizing the economy for war had great consequences not just for the state but for the entire political economy. The "countervailing" powers of the modern mixed economy—big government, big business, big labor, and big farming—all grew in size and scope and took on clearer and somewhat different dimensions and relationships. The military's role in economic decisions increased. And by demonstrating that massive deficit spending could fire an economy from depression to prosperity, the war brought Keynesian ideas to the heart of American public policy and political debate.

But there remains disagreement about the impact of World War II on the American political economy. Liberals especially have found much to praise in the mixed economy of countervailing power and Keynesian stimuli that evidently produced widely shared prosperity and economic security after the war. Critics on the left, however, have complained of a military-industrial complex that put dominant state power in the hands of the armed forces and big business, while those on the right have often lamented the statism of great power in the central government. And if World War II has not seemed to everyone a Good War in terms of its impact on government and public policy, many scholars have located the foundations of the modern American state and political economy not in the war years but rather in long-standing patterns and dynamics of the American economy and political system.

Managing War Mobilization

The federal government that mobilized the nation for war had changed dramatically in the 1930s during Franklin D. Roosevelt's first two terms as president. The mixed economy of the New Deal regulatory-welfare state had emerged, a state where microeconomic decisions remained chiefly in private hands but where the federal government regulated business, ensured a significant measure of essential economic security, supported unions and collective bargaining, and was by the end of the decade moving toward Keynesian ideas about underwriting prosperity. The government by 1940 was much bigger and more powerful than it had been in 1932.

Yet despite the increased role and capacity of the New Deal

state, it was unprepared for the huge wartime tasks that lay
ahead. Plants had to be built, expanded, or converted to produce war goods. Raw materials and supplies had to be ac-
quired and delivered to those plants according to appropriate
priorities and schedules. Workers had to be matched to production needs. Civilian supplies had to be produced and allo-
cated in a way that did not detract from war production and
that ensured basic equity. Wages and prices had to be brought
under control in order to avoid ruinous inflation. Money had
to be found to finance the enormously expensive process of
war mobilization and production. Each of those tasks alone
was daunting enough; their scope and complex interrelation-
ships amounted to an extraordinary challenge, far beyond
what the New Deal had taken on in the 1930s.

To this challenge the American government rose slowly
and imperfectly, though ultimately successfully. As was typically the case on the American home front, the wartime experience was shaped by attitudes and institutions present at the
outset of the war. A pervasive antistatist ideology wary of too
much power in the central government, a distrust by liberals
of business-dominated policy, and the limitations of existing
federal agencies all helped produce a slow, often stumbling
management of economic mobilization by the government,
especially before Pearl Harbor.

So too did President Roosevelt's attention to politics and
public opinion, his concern with ends more than means, his
readiness to experiment, his reluctance to reveal himself or his
thinking, and his penchant for diluting the power of others so
as to protect his own. But if he was never a tidy administrator,
Roosevelt was generally an effective one, and he proved a successful commander-in-chief as well. And if he was, in the
terms of his political biographer James MacGregor Burns,
sometimes a cagy, narrowly calculating "fox," FDR was often
also a "lion" in pursuing large national purposes. Whatever

his shortcomings as a manager, Roosevelt was an extraordinary leader who during World War II, as during the Great Depression, gave Americans an indispensable sense of confidence.

Reflecting the personal, political, and institutional dynamics of national policymaking as well as the uncertainties of the period from 1939 to 1941, a confusing and complicated succession of agencies emerged between 1939 and 1943. The first set came in the "defense period" before Pearl Harbor and the American entrance into the war. The most important of these were the War Resources Board (WRB) established in 1939, the Advisory Commission to the Council of National Defense (NDAC), organized in 1940, and the Office of Production Management (OPM) and the Supply Priorities and Allocations Board (SPAB), both created in 1941. In 1940 Roosevelt established in the White House the Office for Emergency Management (OEM), which served as a sort of incubator and umbrella for mobilization agencies. The Office of Price Administration and Civilian Supply (OPACS) began in 1941 to address problems of prices and consumer goods. Short-lived, poorly organized and directed, frequently at odds, these initial mobilization agencies nonetheless established precedents and procedures that characterized the management of mobilization throughout the war, including the limits of their power and effectiveness.

Big business and the military had great influence on mobilization. Labor, though with more official power than ever before, nonetheless played essentially a secondary role. It made sense in a number of ways for the administration to turn to businessmen to staff important mobilization agencies. Despite the growth of government in the 1930s, there was no sufficiently large, expert, and experienced civil service bureaucracy to mobilize and manage the wartime economy. Businessmen, particularly from large corporations, had obvious experience

and know-how. And as he sought consensus behind mobilization before Pearl Harbor, FDR understood that involving
business executives in the process might be politically wise.
Final authority over procurement and contracts lay with the
military, however, and typically the mobilization agencies
themselves could not control or coerce. Often they could not
even coordinate effectively.

Especially before Pearl Harbor, the mobilization agencies
found many large industries reluctant to convert to defense
production. Manufacturers did not wish to forgo the growing
domestic market for consumer goods, and, remembering
slack capacity in the 1930s, they feared overbuilding for defense production that would leave them later with empty factories and large debts. The crucial steel and automobile
industries, in particular, reflected this version of the "depression psychosis" that hung over wartime America. Although
auto assembly lines were needed to produce planes and tanks,
automakers hoarded materials and turned out a million more
cars in 1941 than in 1939. The steel industry journal *Iron Age*
in 1940 and 1941 consistently opposed conversion to military
production and groused about supposedly socialist New Deal
schemes to promote government ownership and controls.

From the beginning, mobilization agencies used the carrot
rather than the stick to entice conversion and expansion for
defense production. The government provided subsidies, low-
cost loans, and quick tax write-offs to businesses that would
invest in production facilities. Contracts were written to guar-
antee manufacturers their cost of production plus a fixed
profit (the "cost-plus" arrangement). The Defense Plant
Corporation spent billions building needed war production
facilities, which were then leased at low rates to private corporations and sold to them at bargain prices at the end of the war.
According to Secretary of War Henry L. Stimson, a Republican appointed by Roosevelt in June 1940, "If you are going to

try to go to war, or to prepare for war, in a capitalist country, you have got to let business make money out of the process or business won't work." From the beginning, financial assistance and contracts went especially to large established industrial firms and to emerging giants in aircraft and electronics. Of $175 billion in prime war contracts awarded from 1940 to 1944, more than half went to just thirty-three firms.

The process and patterns of contract distribution established before Pearl Harbor persisted through the war. They reflected the aims and personnel of the mobilization agencies and the influence of the military procurement officers who awarded contracts. The primary purpose of the defense contracts was to ensure speedy, high-quality, high-capacity production of war goods. It seemed reasonable, even imperative, to meet these needs by suspending competitive bidding and allowing military procurement officers—many of them newly commissioned from corporate America—to turn to established and emerging large firms with requisite experience, plant capacity, research departments, technical ability, management talent, and skilled labor. Similarly, the "dollar-a-year" men—lawyers, financiers, and executives from such industrial giants as U.S. Steel, General Motors, and General Electric—who came to Washington to staff the mobilization agencies turned naturally to the firms and the corporate officers with whom they had done business before. Under Secretary of War Robert P. Patterson claimed that "we had to take industrial America as we found it." Military procurement officers and businessmen also helped persuade the administration to forgo antitrust efforts during the war so as not to antagonize business leaders or disrupt production.

America's entry into the war in December 1941 galvanized mobilization agencies, the production of war goods, and the management of the economy, but largely along lines already established. In January 1942 Roosevelt created the War Production Board (WPB), headed by Donald Nelson, a Sears, Roebuck executive. Designed to exercise general responsibility over the economy in order to effect conversion to war production, restrict nonessential economic activity, and coordinate materials and production priorities, WPB's power and effectiveness were limited from the beginning. Partly the problem was with Nelson himself—a pleasant, well-intentioned man who was not sufficiently decisive. But the larger failures lay with the institutional framework and the existing vectors of power. Special problem areas—rubber and petroleum, for example—were given to independent "czars" removed from Nelson's control. Labor did not fall under WPB's domain. In seeking business expansion and conversion, the WPB continued to rely upon incentives rather than control.

Most important, the army and navy continued to award contracts with little regard for available facilities and the supply of labor and materials, resulting in snarls of priorities, raw materials, and production. Steel, copper, and aluminum were especially in short supply, and the WPB's system of preferences and priorities was at first unable to achieve order or efficiency. Ultimately the Controlled Materials Plan was implemented in 1943. This allowed the army and navy to continue to award contracts but gave the WPB control of material allocations and production schedules and helped ease the difficulties.

In 1943 Roosevelt also established a new coordinating agency, the Office of War Mobilization (OWM). Headed by James F. Byrnes, a former senator from South Carolina and Supreme Court justice, the OWM had significant powers of control and coordination, enough for Byrnes to be called the "assistant president." The OWM thus culminated a four-year effort to organize economic mobilization. Generally siding with big business and the military in their contests with liberals and spokesmen for small business, the OWM was succeeded in late 1944 by the Office of War Mobilization and Reconversion (OWMR), also under Byrnes, as the government looked ahead to demobilization.

Besides industrial production, other mobilization needs and problems gave rise to a myriad of agencies that at times made the New Deal look simple and small. The War Food Administration, for example, sought to coordinate the production and distribution of foodstuffs. Agricultural production was enhanced by the success of the powerful farm bloc in Congress, speaking especially for big farmers and organized agribusiness, in preventing a low ceiling on farm prices. Like big business, big farming, which was represented in government councils by Farm Bureau Federation officials as well as the congressional farm bloc, profited economically from the war and enhanced its political clout.

In dealing with labor, two mobilization issues were especially important: how to keep strikes from snarling production, and how to match workers with essential jobs. Work stoppages became a major problem in 1941 when industrial expansion led workers to seek higher wages and better conditions and unions to seek recognition and protection of its members. The National Defense Mediation Board, created in March 1941, had no real power. Some 4,300 work stoppages occurred that year, involving 2.4 million workers and costing 23 million lost days of work—totals comparable to those of the turbulent labor years of 1919 and 1937.

Soon after Pearl Harbor, FDR negotiated a no-strike/no-lockout agreement with unions and management and then established the National War Labor Board (NWLB) to head off labor strife that might impair the war effort. For a variety of reasons, including worker patriotism, strikes and stoppages fell off sharply in 1942. By the end of the war the NWLB had imposed settlements in some 20,000 wage disputes affecting some 20 million workers, and had approved 415,000 wage agreements. In several dozen instances the government took over plants shut down by work stoppages. The NWLB also helped union membership grow by some two-thirds during the war and aided workers in gaining better working conditions and higher wages.

But many workers and some unions continued to have real grievances: though new fringe benefits helped many workers, wages tended to lag behind prices and profits; manpower controls threatened to prevent workers in specified jobs from seeking better positions and higher pay elsewhere; and management practices in a number of plants seemed capricious or unfair. While wages were controlled, Congress in 1943 rejected Roosevelt's effort to equalize "sacrifice" and cap individual salaries at $25,000 (some $200,000 in 1990 dollars). The no-strike pledge seemed to deprive workers of their chief weapon, but union leaders did not wish to violate it and risk losing influence in government agencies, inflaming antilabor attitudes in Congress and among the public, or seeming ungrateful to the Roosevelt administration. For both patriotic and self-interested reasons, labor wanted to be on the team, to ensure maximum production and minimal disruption of the war effort. Thus union leaders rarely sanctioned strikes, and when unauthorized "wildcat" strikes broke out after 1942 typically did their best to end them.

Work stoppages, largely wildcat strikes, nonetheless increased to some 3,800 in 1943, involving more than twice as many workers (2 million) as in 1942 and four times as many lost man-days (13.5 million). The most significant labor dispute in 1943 came in the bituminous coal industry, where nearly half a million miners struck on four different occasions during the year. They had real grievances: dreadful working conditions, low pay, and arbitrary work and pay rules. They also had a leader, John L. Lewis, who was accustomed to challenging Roosevelt, ignoring public opinion, and going his own way. Each time the workers walked out, the government seized the mines, but late in the year FDR ordered Interior Secretary Harold Ickes to arrange for a contract acceptable to Lewis. Although it stopped short of giving the miners all they wanted, the agreement was sufficient to keep the crucial coal industry working until the end of the war.

Wartime strikes antagonized the public and the conservative Seventy-eighth Congress, which in 1943 enacted over Roosevelt's veto the War Labor Disputes Act, known as the Smith-Connally Act after its principal sponsors. The legislation required unions to give formal notice of a strike, mandated a thirty-day cooling-off period, provided penalties for illegal work stoppages, and enhanced presidential power to seize war plants. It also prohibited union contributions to political campaigns. Although never as harmful as many union leaders feared, the Smith-Connally Act, a precursor to the Taft-Hartley Act of 1947, restricted both the economic and political activity of unions and reflected the ambiguous position of organized labor in the wartime political economy.

While the NWLB and Smith-Connally sought to prevent strikes from disrupting production, the principal agency concerned with managing the labor supply was the War Manpower Commission (WMC). The supply of workers was at first not a problem because of the high levels of unemployment still existing in 1940. But as the armed forces expanded dramatically and production needs rose, labor shortages and turnover began to appear, as did labor hoarding and pirating by some firms. The WMC was established in 1942 to address such problems. But though the WMC and the labor leaders on it seemed to have considerable power, including supervision of the Selective Service system and overall responsibility for manpower allocation, the agency never had control over the size of the military and had only marginal influence over civilian manpower priorities and allocations. With the establishment of the Office of War Mobilization in 1943, the WMC largely lost what power it had over manpower policy, though with other agencies it made some progress in rationalizing the labor market and funneling workers where they were most needed.

Besides again revealing the relative power of labor, business, and the military in wartime mobilization, the story of labor supply also underlines the general reluctance of policy-makers and the American people to allow the government coercive controls except as a last resort. Recurrently through the war, some in government and the military, including FDR, wanted a "work or fight" national service policy, or a "labor draft" policy. Labor opposed such coercion, all the more because it was advocated by some as a punitive response to strikes and labor unrest. On this issue labor was able to have its way, partly because business and conservatives also feared such government power, partly because a national service policy never seemed essential and thus lay outside the wartime consensus.

However slow and fumbling it was, whatever it often lacked in efficiency and equity, however much it depended on voluntarism, enticements, and even luck instead of central direction and controls, the American mobilization effort ultimately succeeded. The sheer capacity of the American economy and the ingenuity and industriousness of managers and workers largely accounted for that, but government agencies played their part too. From 1939 to 1944 the Gross National Product more than doubled (corrected for inflation, it increased by about two-thirds); the proportion of output given over to war goods soared from 2 percent to 40 percent by 1943; and by 1944 the United States was producing 60 percent of Allied munitions and 40 percent of the world's arms.

Managing the Civilian Economy

Prodigious though American production was during the war, it did not provide enough civilian goods to satisfy the home-front demand created by full-employment prosperity. Taxes, war bonds, and voluntary savings did not siphon enough spending power from the economy to prevent a dangerous "inflationary gap" between disposable income and available consumer goods. A system of wage, price, and rent controls was thus essential to combat inflation. Because wartime material and production priorities produced shortages in a variety of consumer goods, and because higher incomes and price controls made such goods affordable, a rationing system was needed to ensure equitable access to many essential or desirable items.

Management of the civilian economy was in some ways more difficult than mobilizing defense production—and a good deal more unpopular. It entailed government controls over prices, wages, supplies, and spending; it seemed to many to deny a fundamental American right to make and spend money without limit; and it bred a widespread and sometimes justified perception of inequity and favoritism. While everyone could agree on the need to check inflation, farmers and manufacturers disliked controls on *their* prices, workers on *their* wages, landlords on *their* rents.

The related problems of how to manage prices and supplies became pressing as early as April 1941 when Roosevelt established the Office of Price Administration and Civilian Supply (OPACS) under Leon Henderson, a pugnacious and often impolitic New Dealer. Like other agencies before Pearl Harbor, OPACS lacked power and was at best marginally effective. With wholesale prices rising a dangerous 13 percent just between March and September 1941, Roosevelt in August replaced OPACS with the Office of Price Administration (OPA), also headed by Henderson. Given authority by Congress early in 1942 to set maximum prices for a wide range of consumer goods, OPA also came to supervise rationing of civilian supplies in an arrangement worked out with the War Production Board.

Despite this greater administrative clarity and power, effective price-control policy was not in place for more than a year. To curtail rapidly rising prices, the OPA in April 1942 issued its General Maximum Price Regulation (known in the wartime climate as General Max), which froze most prices at the highest level reached in March 1942. Not covering farm goods (exempted by Congress from price controls until they reached 110 percent of "parity"—the 1909–1914 ratio between agricultural and industrial prices that was the basis of New Deal farm price supports) or wages (which did not fall under OPA's purview), General Max also failed to stabilize prices on consumer goods. Inventive businesses found ways around it—by slight changes in packaging, style, content, or quality, for example, that allowed them to claim that a product was new and did not fall under the price freeze. For their part, consumers bought what they could in advance of anticipated shortages and thus drove prices up. Consumer prices rose 18 percent from 1941 to 1943.

Better and more effective policy soon emerged in the fight against inflation. Wage controls provided an important part of the solution. In July 1942 the National War Labor Board announced its "Little Steel" formula (so called because it was worked out in response to wage demands at smaller steel companies) that allowed a 15 percent increase in hourly wage rates from January 1, 1941, to offset the rise in living costs between then and May 1942. The Little Steel formula did not cap labor income—overtime and incentive pay, job upgrades, and new fringe benefits all increased labor's compensation package and spending power—and the NWLB was at first permitted to grant larger increases as needed to correct inequities. But for all that it was criticized and circumvented, the Little Steel formula did help brake rising wage rates and thus check inflation.

In October 1942 FDR brought administrative order and greater effectiveness to the control of inflation when he persuaded Congress to pass the Economic Stabilization Act and arranged for Supreme Court Justice James F. Byrnes to leave the Court in order to head the new Office of Economic Stabilization (OES). The OES had authority to control farm prices and oversee wages; and by putting Byrnes's office in the White House, FDR, who remembered vividly the 60 percent rise in prices during World War I, signaled his resolve to check inflation. He did so again in April 1943 with a "hold-the-line" order on wages and prices.

By 1943 inflation had been brought under control. While the consumer price index had risen by some 25 percent from 1939 to 1943, it increased by only about 4 percent from 1943 to 1945. Some prices and incomes rose much more than others, and the price index did not reveal a number of hidden price increases—such as lower quality, the elimination of discounts, services, and less expensive lines, and higher prices on the active wartime black market. Still, the fight against inflation was remarkably successful in the second half of the war. And while price controls were never wildly popular, polls showed that more than 90 percent of the public approved of them.

The other part of OPA's mission—rationing—was more effective and less popular. In 1942 the OPA implemented ten major rationing programs, and more came later. The public generally acknowledged the need to ration consumer goods that were in short supply. But even though consumer spending, especially on foodstuffs, actually increased during the war, Americans chafed under limitations on their purchases.

Rationing seemed counter to American individualism and dreams of abundance—and was even more galling for preventing purchases just when people could afford them after a decade of hard times. It was especially irritating and frustrating that some of the rationed goods were at the heart of the good life as most Americans defined it. In order to conserve scarce rubber supplies, gasoline was rationed and automobile driving restricted. Canned foods were rationed to save precious tin, and meat was rationed in order to meet military and Allied needs. Sugar, coffee, butter, shoes, and other staple items were also added to the list of rationed goods.

Many wartime Americans were sure that shortages were caused by foul-ups in Washington, and that rationing simply aggravated the problem. A major target of complaint was OPA red tape. Ration books, coupons, and colored stamps for foodstuffs and other items; the A, B, C priority sticker system for gasoline; special certificates to purchase selected items; constant and confusing recalculations of the "point system" for different items; and uncertain rules for allocating coupon books and rationed goods to families—all these became an unwelcome part of wartime life. People did not need coupons to eat in restaurants, which had their own point system—and the more expensive restaurants evidently turned often to the black market for supplies of meat for their customers. Because rationing boards were run by local citizens, they gained a certain prestige and authority; but they were also prey to pressure and favoritism—or at least the suspicion of them—and rationing and rationing boards operated differently in different parts of the nation. In Washington, OPA became one of the most politicized and lobbied of agencies, from the beginning the target of politicians and special interests.

Many home-front Americans simply did not comply with rationing and price controls, at least not all the time. In addition to sometimes using counterfeit ration coupons, otherwise respectable citizens and merchants were involved in the black market, where controlled goods could be bought in amounts beyond the ration allocation at prices often well above established ceilings. One study indicated that during the war one in fifteen businesses was charged with illegal operations and that one in five received warnings. Twenty-five percent of the public thought using the black market was sometimes justified.

OPA was especially unpopular in 1942. After its programs were blamed for Democratic setbacks in that year's elections, Leon Henderson was cashiered and replaced by the much more politic Chester Bowles, a millionaire advertising man who went on to a distinguished career in politics and public service. As price controls were given teeth and as rationing became more familiar, the antipathy against OPA diminished, at least until V-J day when it flared again. The anti-inflation program was an important success and the rationing program helped wage and price controls work and promoted an equitable distribution of scarce goods. But the management of the civilian economy was much more an administrative and economic success than it was a political one.

MANAGING THE BUDGET

World War II cost an extraordinary amount of money. In all, the federal government spent more than $300 billion during the war—almost twice as much money as it had in its entire previous history from George Washington's first term to the beginning of the war. Federal expenditures exploded from $8.9 billion in 1939 to $98.4 billion in 1945; and average annual federal expenses from Pearl Harbor to the end of 1945, roughly $75 billion, exceeded the entire national income of 1939. Even when corrected for an inflation rate of some 30 percent, these were stunning increases.

From the beginning the obvious question was how to finance the war—in particular, how much to pay out of current revenues and how much to cover by borrowing or printing money. The financing of the war, moreover, was connected to the problem of inflation. To the degree that the government could finance the war by taxes, and thus take money out of the hands of consumers, effective demand could be dampened and inflation checked. Borrowing, especially by means of war bonds, was another way to siphon off purchasing power in the short run and would for individuals be a source of savings; but it would also run up the federal debt and have a larger inflationary impact.

Roosevelt strongly preferred to finance the war by taxes. But he met opposition from the public, from business, and from Congress, none of whom wanted heavier or more extensive taxation. Ultimately taxes paid for just under half the wartime expenses—less than Roosevelt had wanted, but substantially more than the one-third financed out of current revenues during World War I. Both the shaping and the shape of wartime tax policy shed substantial light on the policymaking and political economy of wartime America.

In 1942 Congress and the administration wrestled over the first wartime revenue act. The bill sent to Capitol Hill by the White House in March was intended to be both progressive and anti-inflationary, with high personal incomes, corporate income, excess profits, and estate, gift, and excise taxes bearing the brunt of the increases. Congress balked, preferring much smaller increases in those areas and a national sales tax to raise money and check inflation. Roosevelt was able to stave off the regressive sales tax, but at the price of a lower tax bill on high incomes and profits and a substantial extension of the personal income tax to include incomes over $624.

Perhaps the most important feature of the 1942 Revenue Act, and indeed of the new wartime tax structure, was that a much larger proportion of the public paid income taxes. Between 1939 and 1942 the number of taxable returns soared from 4 million to 28 million. With so many more people paying taxes, a payroll deduction scheme looked increasingly appealing as a simpler and easier way to collect them. But if withholding were to begin in 1943, taxpayers would have money taken out of their pay for 1943 taxes at the same time they had to find money to pay their 1942 tax bill. The solution was proposed by Beardsley Ruml, chairman of the New York Federal Reserve Bank and treasurer of R. H. Macy and Company. Ruml suggested simply forgiving taxpayers most of their 1942 tax obligations, beginning payroll deductions in 1943, and thus having collections for 1943, rather than the 1942 tax bill, provide government revenue in the new year. Likening it to daylight savings time, Ruml said the plan would just move "the tax clock forward, and cost the Treasury nothing until Judgment Day." And on Judgment Day, one politician observed, "no one will give a damn." Roosevelt opposed the Ruml plan, which he saw as a windfall to the rich, an avoidance of responsibility, and a loss of important revenue, but Congress approved it.

The 1943 legislation did not raise as much money as the administration had wanted in order to enhance revenues and check inflation. Accordingly FDR asked the Congress for another $10.5 billion in taxes. But though Americans were paying taxes at a lower rate than was the case in other nations at war, many in Congress saw that sum as an "unbearable burden" and instead passed a much smaller revenue package— some $2 billion in new taxes, with provisions favoring various business interests. In February 1944 FDR angrily vetoed the measure, calling it "wholly ineffective" and "not a tax bill but a tax relief bill providing relief not for the needy but for the greedy." Affronted by FDR's challenge to its authority, and calling his preferences "oppressive to tax payers," Congress overwhelmingly overrode the veto. Reflecting the wartime conflict between a conservative Congress and the liberal administration, the episode marked the first time in the nation's history that Congress had overridden a presidential veto of a revenue bill.

Wartime policy had profound implications for the nation's tax structure and the financing of government operations. Whereas relatively few Americans had paid income taxes before the war, most full-time workers did during—and after—the war. In all, the number of taxable tax returns rose from some 4 million in 1939 to nearly 43 million in 1945. The income tax took 3.4 percent of all personal income in 1941 and 12.2 percent of the much larger incomes of 1945. During the war, moreover, personal income tax receipts supplanted corporate income taxes as the largest source of federal revenue. The new tax structure had great impact on economic policy. Withholding taxes permitted the speedy impact on consumer spending of raising or lowering taxes, while the broadened tax base and the much larger individual (and corporate) tax receipts going to Washington helped underwrite the higher levels of federal spending that began with the war.

But taxes paid for less than half the costs of the war. The remainder was financed by borrowing or printing money. Borrowing, like taxing, also aimed to control inflation, and toward that end the Treasury Department conducted seven loan drives during the war. In promoting its bonds, Treasury hoped to increase public involvement in the war effort, channel funds from consumption to savings, and help pay for the war. In all, war loan drives took in some $135 billion, though a disappointingly small part of that sum came from individuals, who purchased only about a quarter of the war bonds. For the most part the loans were financed by banks, insurance companies, and large corporations.

The most important aspect of wartime borrowing was not its means but rather its size and impact. The national debt rose more than fivefold, from some $49 billion in 1941 to $259 billion in 1945 (from 39 to 121 percent of GNP). Wartime spending not only produced the goods to defeat the Axis but also underwrote full-employment prosperity. The war in that way served as a kind of economic laboratory, evidently confirming the argument of the British economist John Maynard Keynes that deficit spending could produce prosperity.

Keynes explained the dynamics of market economies in terms of aggregate demand, which included consumer spending, private investment, and government spending. If there were insufficient aggregate demand, an economy might lag well below full capacity. In this analysis there was a clear—a compensating—role for government spending. Should there be insufficient consumer spending and private investment, government expenditures had to provide the balance to achieve full-production prosperity. But if government spent more by raising taxes, that would take money out of the hands of consumers or investors; for government spending to have its largest impact, it should be deficit spending, over and above what the government took in.

By the late 1930s an influential coterie of New Deal economists had concluded that massive deficit spending could stimulate the economy back to full production and full employment—and that the spending itself could be for such liberal programs as welfare, public housing, and health. In a "compensatory state," government spending could make up for inadequate private spending and investment and in so doing underwrite both prosperity and reform. Still, most economists and policymakers remained wedded to the old doctrine that considered deficit spending a dangerous fiscal expedient.

Then came the war, and with it massive deficits, and with the deficits booming, full-production, full-employment prosperity. Unemployment fell from 15 percent in 1940 to an almost unbelievable 1 percent in 1944. The case for Keynesian economics could scarcely have been made with greater force. The study of economics and the application of economic theory to public policy were transformed. As a result, liberals generally came to appreciate and advocate the compensatory state. And not just liberals and New Dealers, but many moderates and businessmen became persuaded of the importance of fiscal policy and the role that taxing and spending could play in the performance of the economy.

Important differences of opinion, however, remained. Moderates and business preferred to incur deficits by cutting taxes and putting spending decisions in the hands of consumers, investors, and businessmen. Wartime government spending was one thing, but peacetime spending might go for all of those social projects that many businessmen and others opposed. Liberals, by contrast, preferred a different version of Keynesianism. Progressive taxation could take idle money from the wealthy and help put it in the hands of poorer people who would spend it; and government spending could go toward liberal social programs and projects.

Wartime spending and its impact thus helped change economic doctrine and debate. Keynesian ideas became central to the liberal agenda, were accepted at least in part by most economists and many businessmen, and became fundamental to the political economy of wartime and postwar America. Like the other aspects of economic policy during the war—mobilization, managing the civilian economy, taxation—wartime government spending had a large and lasting impact on the nation. Like them too, however, it continued prewar trends and developments in politics and policymaking as well as creating new ones.

THE POLITICAL ECONOMY OF WAR—AND PEACE

Not long after World War II, John Kenneth Galbraith provided in *American Capitalism* his influential description of the modern American political economy. It was, he said, neither the government-controlled economy that conservatives decried nor the big-business-dominated economy that liberals feared; and it was a good deal more stable and solid than either camp recognized. According to Galbraith, modern American capitalism was a system of "countervailing" powers, in which the great power of big business was countered by other sources of power, typically created and supported by the state. Thus public policy supported organized labor and organized farming, and it also protected unorganized workers by means of social insurance, minimum wages, and the like. Government fiscal policy—taxing and spending—helped underwrite prosperity and economic stability. Galbraith did not assign World War II a major role in creating the new American capitalism. In his account the Great Depression and the New Deal loomed far larger, though trends could be traced back decades earlier. Galbraith's account dovetails nicely with the "organizational" interpretation of historians who have stressed the importance of large, centralized, bureaucratic organizations in modern America. They would agree that World War II did not create but rather confirmed and crystallized the organizational society, reinforcing trends and patterns under way for a half-century and more and accelerated in the New Deal years.

But if World War II was not really a fundamental turning point in the development of the modern American political economy, it was an important and in some ways a decisive era for economic ideas, structure, and policy. Certainly the experience of war had a large impact on the perceptions and agenda

of American liberals. Before the war many liberals had
wanted thoroughgoing national planning and economic controls in a greatly enhanced administrative and regulatory
state. The dreadful performance of the American economy in
the 1930s and the human toll of the depression produced pessimism about the capacity of the private sector and a determination that the public sector must have enlarged powers of
regulation and coordination to ensure economic efficiency and
equity.

By the end of the war, however, most liberals had changed
their minds and had come to advocate the compensatory state
where government used its macroeconomic powers of spending and taxing rather than its microeconomic powers of planning and control. The mobilization agencies had been
dominated by big business and the military, which made liberals fear all the more their "capture" in peacetime. The wartime experience had in any case made even more plain the
complexity of the economy and the difficulties of federal
micromanagement. And wartime expansion had demonstrated the remarkable capacity of the American economy and
the ability of fiscal policy to achieve full-production prosperity
in a way that was far easier politically and seemed more effective economically than planning and controls. As most liberals
understood, and some lamented, the embrace of a compensatory state involved a substantial shift in both the aims and
means of liberal policy.

But the political economy of wartime and postwar America
saw not only a redefinition of the liberal agenda but also—
and relatedly—an alteration in the dynamics of power, in particular an enhancement of the role of business and the military
in policymaking. The power of the "military-industrial complex" was evident not only in the role of businessmen and military procurement officers in wartime mobilization and in the
gains made by the large and emerging defense industries but

also in the processes of managing the economy. Thus mobilization was achieved not by fiat but by enticements to private enterprise.

Building upon the wartime experience, government after the war found it far easier politically and just as effective economically to spend for military purposes rather than for domestic social reform and social welfare. It also proved easier to unbalance the budget by lowering taxes than by spending more on domestic programs. Rather than the liberal Keynesian program of deficit spending to underwrite reform, prosperity, and economic security, postwar fiscal policy was more an amalgam of national-security "military Keynesianism" and cautious, tax-cutting "commercial Keynesianism." The compensatory state of wartime and postwar America reflected not only widely shared national priorities during World War II and the cold war but also the political and policymaking powers of business, the military, and their advocates in government and in Congress.

These powers were also evident in the reconversion policy that connected wartime and postwar America. Liberals wanted well-planned, early, and incremental reconversion to peacetime production. They sought to protect small business and workers as war production fell off, and favored a major part for labor in reconversion policy. On each count, reconversion took a different course. Partly this was because of the influence of big business and the military, partly because Congress, a conservative anchor against New Deal reform throughout the war, played a crucial role in shaping reconversion policy.

In what became known as "the war within a war," the struggle over reconversion began in 1943 and involved especially issues of timing and process. The big war contractors did not want prospective competitors allowed a head start in resuming civilian production. They also desired generous policies for contract termination and disposition of government-owned plants. Understandably insisting that nothing hamper war production, the military wanted to delay reconversion at least until Germany was defeated. Reconversion was largely coordinated by the Office of War Mobilization (OWM) and its successor, the Office of War Mobilization and Reconversion (OWMR). As during the mobilization phase, agency decisions generally coincided with the preferences of business and the military. Protected against reconversion by potential competitors, big business was also helped by policies on contract termination and disposal of "surplus" government-owned plants that further entrenched their economic size and power. Most plants were sold cheaply to war contractors and other corporate giants with the assets to purchase them. And, as labor complained, the so-called "human side of reconversion," including the training and placement of discharged war workers and returning veterans, took second place to contract termination, surplus property disposal, and the rest of business reconversion.

When the war ended in the summer of 1945, the dismantling of wartime agencies started at once, and reconversion proceeded chiefly by private initiative and continuing public subsidy rather than by government direction. The new liberal agenda went largely unfulfilled in the early postwar era, with the Full Employment Bill drafted by liberal Keynesians becoming the watered-down Employment Act of 1946 and with the chief labor legislation being the union-opposed Taft-Hartley Act of 1947. Meanwhile, military spending and the national security state, partly ratified in the National Security Act of 1947, helped to underwrite postwar prosperity.

The political economy of wartime and postwar America was thus in significant ways a warfare state as much as a welfare state, geared to national security as well as to economic security. The New Deal had not, to be sure, been repealed, nor had the power to make economic policy been concentrated in the Pentagon or corporate boardrooms. The New Deal regulatory-welfare state remained largely intact, and for all the power of business, conservatives, and the military in wartime economic policy, liberals retained substantial influence. But the mixed economy of wartime and postwar America was characterized by a military-industrial complex as well as by Galbraith's countervailing powers—and some would say that a "big military" now had power rivaling or exceeding that of big business, big labor, and big farming. And while government spending underwrote wartime and postwar prosperity, the fiscal stimulus was more a combination of business and military Keynesianism than it was the liberal Keynesianism of progressive taxation and compensatory spending on social reform. Because of its production record and the role of "dollar-a-year" businessmen in government, moreover, big business regained much of the reputation lost during the depression; and the restored image of business was part of the more general resurgence of conservatism that made 1930s-style social reform more difficult to achieve, as the wartime and postwar Congresses made clear.

In all of this, World War II had a substantial impact and legacy. It significantly enhanced the power of the state, gave somewhat different and clearer form to the American mixed economy, and further crystallized the organizational society. Yet the political economy of wartime and postwar America was in important ways a familiar one, and the nature of the American state had not been transformed. The New Deal had expanded the role of government but it never really surmounted—and in part shared—the conservative antistatism of the American political culture that powerfully reemerged in the late 1930s. Businessmen had played important roles in New Deal economic agencies—and in leading opposition to the New Deal. The "military-industrial complex" had been developing since World War I or before. The liberal conversion to Keynesianism had begun before the war, as had the realization of some influential businessmen that fiscal policy was central to the economy's performance.

Whether such outcomes and patterns should be judged good or bad depended—and still depends—on the perspectives and preferences of those judging. But what almost everyone then and since could agree on was that the economic mobilization for war, whatever its impact on the government and the political economy, fueled a dual victory over the Axis abroad and over the Great Depression at home, and in so doing provided a buoyant sense of national accomplishment and potential. In that way, surely, World War II seemed a Good War.

3

Victory at Home and Abroad

WARTIME AMERICA was the fabled "Arsenal of Democracy," whose scientists and factory workers were as important to the defeat of the Axis as were its soldiers and sailors, and whose industrial and technological might made the United States the economic and military colossus of the globe. But economic mobilization also brought full employment, fat pay envelopes, and rising expectations. Crucial to the double victory over the Axis and the Great Depression, the "miracles of mobilization" enhanced confidence in the nation's institutions and its large organizations.

Even here, where the story has long seemed so clear and compelling, there is debate about the impact of the war and the nature of the wartime experience. Some historians have emphasized how mobilization got off to a slow and stumbling start, never achieved full capacity, rewarded especially the already well-off and powerful, and reinforced the hold of large, organized interests in American life. In these ways and others, the argument runs, wartime America displayed powerful continuities.

The economic historian Robert Higgs has challenged even the reality of wartime prosperity. While acknowledging that the war laid groundwork for postwar prosperity by increasing income and savings and raising expectations, he contends that the idea of wartime prosperity must be discarded. Rather than a consumer-oriented market economy, wartime America had a command economy where military employment and production yielded misleading figures of economic well-being; true prosperity with high levels of civilian employment, production, and consumption did not occur until after the war. In this view, moreover, hidden inflation, deteriorating quality, scarce goods, long working hours, and wartime inconveniences and dislocations all invalidate the conventional understanding that "economically speaking, Americans had never had it so good." This provocative argument involves a sharp contrast indeed to notions of the Good War and its large and beneficial impact on American life.

THE DUAL VICTORY

The performance of the wartime economy was extraordinary in its dimensions and its consequences, all the more so in view of the dismal experience of the 1930s. From 1940 to 1944 industrial output increased by more than 15 percent annually, compared with 7 percent annually during World War I. The Gross National Product more than doubled, growing from $91 billion in 1939 to $126 billion in 1941, to $193 billion in 1943, to $214 billion in 1945. (Measured in "constant dollars" to correct for wartime inflation, the GNP rose from $91 billion in 1939 to roughly $150 billion in both 1944 and 1945—a remarkable real increase of some two-thirds in just five years.)

A number of factors underlay this remarkable economic expansion. For one thing, the American economy had considerable slack at the outset of the war. In labor supply, in plant capacity, in raw materials, wartime expansion was largely a result of mobilizing underutilized productive resources. For another, labor, material, and other resources were converted to war production or redirected from other sectors of the economy after 1939. Finally, wartime production was fueled by a remarkable 25 percent rise in productivity, largely the result of new technologies and capital equipment, economies of scale, better management of productive resources, and the sense of common cause. American output per hour of work was roughly twice that of the Germans, five times that of the Japanese.

The result was the fabled production prodigies of wartime America. During the war the United States produced some 5,600 merchant ships, 80,000 landing craft, 100,000 tanks and armored cars, 300,000 airplanes, 370,000 large artillery weapons, 2.4 million military trucks, 2.6 million machine guns, 20 million small arms, 434 million tons of steel, 41 billion rounds of ammunition, and 6 million tons of bombs. Aircraft and ship production both were more than ten times higher in 1943 than in 1940, munitions manufacture twenty-seven times higher. Farm output overall increased by 17 percent, spurred by an increase of one-third in farm productivity according to one measure.

New and nascent industries and a variety of war-related products took off during the war. Wartime technology and fabrication laid foundations for postwar growth in aerospace, electronics, plastics, chemicals, communications, and other industries. Radar, proximity fuses, and other technological breakthroughs helped win the war, though no doubt the most impressive technological and engineering accomplishment was the Manhattan Project that produced the atomic bomb. Japanese control of Southeast Asia provoked a remarkably successful synthetic rubber program, financed and administered by government, that made the United States essentially self-sufficient. But the needs of war elicited other new developments as well—DDT to combat malaria-carrying mosquitoes in the South Pacific, for example, and crucial new advances in blood plasma, antibiotics, and other pharmaceuticals. In such scientific and technological advances, the government and the military increasingly relied upon and provided funding for university research and scientists, relationships that would expand after the war and continue to influence the role and structure of American universities. Rather than a "military-industrial complex," in fact, wartime and postwar America perhaps more accurately had a military-industrial-scientific-academic complex.

The United States also helped provide the sinews of war for its Allies. Beginning in 1941 the nation spent nearly $50 billion in Lend-Lease assistance, first to Britain and then to the Soviet Union and others. The United States supplied roughly one-quarter of the arms used by the British. While the Soviets relied much less on American war materiel—less than 5 percent of their total—they depended more on foodstuffs and received about $10 billion in Lend-Lease assistance. By 1944 some 60 percent of Allied munitions and 40 percent of the world's arms were being produced by the United States.

Despite such achievements the American productive effort during World War II has sometimes been exaggerated and even romanticized. If the United States ultimately produced twice as much as the Axis nations, American national income before the war had been almost twice the combined national incomes of Germany, Italy, and Japan. Remarkable though wartime economic expansion was, economic growth from 1941 to 1944–1945 was comparable in rate to the peacetime expansion from 1921 to 1924–1925. Never did the United States devote itself to war production as fully as the other combatants; where some two-fifths of American GNP went to the war effort, half and more did so in Britain and Germany. From 1939 to 1943 real consumer spending (corrected for inflation) rose by 12 percent in the United States while falling by 30 percent in England. As another example, women were employed at only about half the rate as in Britain and the Soviet

Union (though at roughly the same rate as in Germany, which experienced little increase in working women).

American military equipment was sometimes inferior and inadequate, not up to the performance of Japanese and especially German weapons. Early in the Pacific war, American fighter planes could not match those of the Japanese, and American torpedoes failed with distressing frequency. The American antitank bazooka, semiautomatic rifles, mortars, and small-arms ammunition all fell below German standards. American tanks, typically underarmored and underarmed, were inferior on both counts to German tanks. The Sherman tank, America's principal battle tank, was nicknamed the "Ronson" (a best-selling cigarette lighter) because of its dismaying propensity for going up in flames when hit.

Some manufacturing initiatives never produced weapons in the quality or quantity promised or expected. One example was the huge and highly publicized Willow Run bomber plant built by Henry Ford; the first B-24 Liberator delivered by the automobile engineers was called by Charles Lindbergh "the worst piece of metal aircraft construction I have ever seen." Despite improvements in quality, the Liberator was inferior to the B-17 Flying Fortress, and Willow Run failed to meet its production schedules and goals. Although improved design, new technologies, and above all the enormous productive capacity of the United States ultimately produced weaponry and firepower that brought victory, the record of American weapons production was not untarnished.

Nor was American aid to the Allies quite as selfless or as decisive as is sometimes depicted. Not only was Lend-Lease begun in part as a last-ditch effort to help England short of an American combat role, but it got under way slowly, carried (to prevent British economic competition) a stipulation that no Lend-Lease product could be used to produce exports, did not apply to all goods exported to the Allies, and was quickly

cut off once the war ended. For the British, Lend-Lease also
involved important concessions to the United States. Allied
cooperation was in any case not a one-way street. The British
stood off Hitler almost single-handedly for more than a year,
provided essential facilities and support for American troops
in Britain, and played a critical role in radar and other important scientific advances. The Soviet Union not only carried the
brunt of the war in Europe from mid-1941 to mid-1944 but
produced the overwhelming majority of its own war materiel.
None of this is to denigrate America's remarkable wartime
mobilization or its vital contribution to victory; but it had limits and did not win the war alone.

The domestic consequences of wartime mobilization have
long seemed as spectacular as the military triumphs. As late as
1940 some eight million workers—15 percent of the labor
force—were still unemployed, and virtually every index reflected the ongoing ravages of the depression. War production
helped end the depression even as it spelled the doom of the
Axis. Unemployment fell to just 5 percent in 1942 and then to
the stunning 1 percent of 1944. With the armed forces expanding to nine million by 1943 and civilian manufacturing employment rising by some six million, the employment problem
of the depression decade was reversed: by 1943 the problem
was how to find workers for all the jobs that needed to be
done. The tasks of locating, training, and placing workers
were, like so many others, accomplished by a sometimes confusing, sometimes inefficient, but ultimately successful combination of public and private efforts. Additional workers came
especially from the unemployed of 1940, from agriculture,
from women, from African Americans, and from a variety of
other workers who had been little utilized before the war.

The war brought rising living standards as well as full employment, for home-front jobs came with higher wages and,

especially in manufacturing, overtime pay. National income and total employee compensation corrected for inflation both rose by some 85 percent from 1939 to 1944. To be sure, rationing and shortages diminished consumer spending, especially on such coveted items as cars and various foods; and even the 30 percent rise in the cost of living did not reflect lowered quality, declining services, diminished choice, the black market, and other hidden costs. But income rose much faster than prices, Americans were fully employed, and overall consumer production and consumer spending grew during the war. Personal savings soared from $3 billion in 1939 to $37 billion ($27 billion in 1939 constant dollars) in 1944. Whatever technical objections might be raised to the idea of wartime prosperity, the war obviously produced economic expansion, full employment, greater purchasing power, and higher living standards. Good times did succeed hard times on the American home front and bred renewed optimism and rising expectations.

The production that brought the dual victory over the Axis and the Great Depression also made the United States the economic powerhouse of the world. While the other major belligerents saw their economies damaged, distorted, and diminished, the United States experienced enormous economic growth and the emergence of major new industries in aircraft, electronics, metals, and synthetics. In raw materials, industrial plant, agricultural production, monetary strength, technology and science, trained manpower, and more, the United States had no peer. In 1947 it produced about half the world's manufactured goods and almost 60 percent of the world's oil and steel, 80 percent of the world's automobiles, and 40 percent of the world's electricity. According to the economic historian Alan S. Milward, "by 1945 the foundations of the United States' economic domination over the next quarter of a century had been secured." In his view, the expansion of the American economy "may have been the most influential consequence of the Second World War for the post-war world."

Wartime success and power reinforced in many Americans a sense of the superiority as well as the strength of American ideas and American institutions. American might and American right seemed intertwined. Proud of their system and accomplishments, many Americans looked to reform and reshape the world. Some, like liberal Vice-President Henry A. Wallace, wanted a sort of international New Deal, a "Century of the Common Man" spread with American power and beneficence to provide freedom, justice, and plenty. Others, like *Time-Life* publisher Henry Luce, also saw the United States as the "powerhouse of the ideals of Freedom and Justice," but called for a seemingly more nationalistic "American Century." Whatever the precise prescription, many shared the sense of the young war correspondent Eric Sevareid who wrote upon returning home that he had left when the United States was "merely the world's hope" and came back to find America "the world's necessity." The United States, he said, might "work greatly to create a world in its own great image."

THE ORGANIZATIONAL SOCIETY

Important to the sense of American strength and possibilities were the increased power and prestige of the large, centralized, bureaucratic organizations, public and private, that characterized the modern American political economy. In the words of the historian Gerald D. Nash, the war both "greatly hastened the development of a more highly organized society in the United States" and "strengthened the faith of millions of Americans in the role of big government, big business, agriculture, and labor unions in dealing with the nation's major problems. Americans thus entered the postwar era with a positive, if somewhat naive, belief in the efficacy of an organizational society."

American business profited enormously from World War II and entered a golden era of expansion and profitability. While total national income, agricultural income, and employee compensation (corrected for inflation) all rose by more than four-fifths from 1939 to 1944, business profits nearly tripled. Various segments of the business community fared differently. As military procurement officers turned to the large firms, and as those firms often hoarded materials and labor or refused to subcontract to smaller concerns, big business did especially well while many small businesses struggled. Ninety-four percent of primary contractors received just 10 percent of the contract dollars; meanwhile the hundred firms that had produced 30 percent of American manufacturing in 1940 accounted for 70 percent of defense contracts by 1943. A sample group of 252 big defense contractors did subcontract about one-third the value of their prime contracts, but three-fourths of that went to other large firms.

Such a skewed distribution of contracts accelerated both the concentration of economic power and ongoing organizational trends within large corporations. Smaller manufacturers with fewer than five hundred employees accounted for just over half of total manufacturing employment in 1939 but won only 22 percent of prime defense contracts and 7 percent of subcontracts, and fell to only 38 percent of manufacturing employment by 1944. By contrast, big firms with ten thousand or more workers employed 13 percent of manufacturing labor in 1939 but more than 30 percent in 1944. The new demands on the nation's industrial giants necessitated further improvements in organizational structure and administrative and managerial techniques to coordinate supply, manufacture, and distribution. Conversion or retooling also sped trends toward diversification, especially in such industries as metals, chemicals, transportation, electronics, and petroleum.

Concerned about small business and its future, Congress established the Smaller War Plants Corporation (SWPC) in 1942, but despite its efforts SWPC was unable to accomplish much. Nor did the special Senate committee headed by Missouri Senator Harry S. Truman to oversee the war effort, or the Smaller War Plants Division of the War Production Board, do much to help small business. Unable to land contracts or use controlled materials and scarce workers, a half-million small businesses failed from 1940 to 1945 by one estimate, or about 20 percent of the 1940 total. Whatever the nation's emotional and rhetorical commitment to small enterprise, and whatever the political concerns about small local industries, the necessities and realities of mobilization—and later of reconversion—tended to work in favor of the established and burgeoning giants.

Yet the story was more complicated than simply damage to small business. The overall business failure rate dropped sharply from 1939 to 1945, and the 1940–1945 average of some thirty failures per ten thousand concerns was less than the rate in the booming 1920s and 1950s. The war also produced roughly a 10 percent increase in the number of manufacturing firms, most of them smaller ones. If small businesses rarely shared in the bonanza of defense contracts, and if many, especially in construction, retail, and service, went under during the war, the rising tides of wartime prosperity (and the trickle down of some war contracts) kept most small businesses afloat, raised a good many to higher levels, and launched new ones. Of 3,500 small plants surveyed by the Office of War Information in 1943, two-thirds said they were doing better than before the war, while just 5 percent feared having to close down.

Nor did big business always profit so disproportionately from the war as some figures suggest. Although large companies dominated war contracts and postwar defense plant and surplus property disposal, the share of manufacturing assets held by the two hundred largest firms held steady at roughly 45 percent from 1941 to 1947. Net profits of small businesses often increased faster than those of the largest firms, and small businesses may have been better positioned and more flexible than large war contractors in meeting changing economic conditions. In his study of small business during the war, Jonathan J. Bean concludes that on balance small manufacturers prospered during the war and were optimistic about the future.

Indeed, the story of conversion, mobilization, and production was a mixed and complicated one from almost any angle. Some business leaders, in large and small firms alike, shrewder or luckier than others, prospered beyond all expectation while others faltered. While many of the nation's established big businesses converted only slowly and reluctantly to war production, such industries as aircraft, shipbuilding, munitions, and electronics eagerly sought war contracts and other forms of government finance and subsidy from the beginning. From United Aircraft and the Electric Boat Company in Connecticut, to the Alabama Dry Dock and Shipbuilding Company in Mobile, to Boeing Aircraft and the Oregon Shipbuilding Corporation in the Pacific Northwest, such firms profited gladly and sometimes hugely from economic mobilization for war.

Shipbuilding and aircraft were largely concentrated in the Sunbelt states of the South and West and produced two of the most storied and dynamic of the wartime entrepreneurs: Andrew Jackson Higgins and Henry J. Kaiser. Higgins's domain was the Gulf South. A colorful figure whom *Fortune* magazine regarded as a combination of Huey Long and Henry

Ford, Higgins had established his name before the war by
building superb boats. Winning both lucrative contracts and
handsome financing from the navy, Higgins Industries built
during the war a variety of small fast craft, including the PT
boats that earned such fame in the Pacific. His shipyards won
enviable reputations for speed, volume, and quality.

But Higgins could not compare to the West Coast's Henry
J. Kaiser as a wartime enterpriser. Hard-driving, inventive,
inspired by a vision for himself and the West, and ready to use
government as a way to achieve that vision, Kaiser had earned
recognition in the 1930s for his work with the Six Companies
consortium in constructing the Boulder, Bonneville, and
Grand Coulee dams. His record, connections, and talents rewarded him handsomely—and also the nation and the
West—during the war. Kaiser Industries won billions of dollars in government contracts for ten different shipyards and
built aircraft carriers and destroyer escorts, tankers and landing craft, troop ships and the "Liberty ships" that became the
war's primary cargo ships.

Using prefabrication as much as possible, Kaiser accounted
for some 30 percent of the entire national shipbuilding effort
in 1943. His mass-production techniques—and his employees' high pay and good benefits, including medical care and
child-care centers—brought astonishing new efficiencies to
ship construction. In 1941 it had taken East Coast shipyards
about a year to build a ten-thousand-ton Liberty ship; by 1942
Kaiser had reduced the time to two months, and by 1944 to
just over two weeks. In one stunning demonstration he built
one of the vessels in four days. Kaiser also entered steel and
metals manufacture and airplane production during the war,
and ultimately employed a quarter of a million workers.

Another industry marked by inventive enterprise and remarkable accomplishment was the manufacture of synthetic
rubber. Rubber was vital to the war effort at home and

abroad, but Japanese control of Southeast Asia cut off some 90 percent of the nation's supply by early 1942. Typically the United States responded slowly to an evident need, but led by "Rubber Czar" William M. Jeffers, the federal government ultimately spent some three-quarters of a billion dollars to build more than fifty plants leased and run by rubber, chemical, and petroleum companies. The output of synthetic rubber leapt from 22,000 tons in 1942 to 230,000 tons in 1943, then to 750,000 tons in 1944—some 90 percent of the nation's requirements.

During and after the war such "miracles of production" prompted much boasting about the virtues of private enterprise. They also restored public esteem for big business. Yet the synthetic rubber industry, like shipbuilding and aircraft and other war production, depended heavily on government assistance. By one estimate, the federal government provided two-thirds of all industrial financing in the 1940–1943 expansion. Subsidies and loans were apportioned in much the same way as contracts—to the established and upcoming giants. Talent, initiative, and enterprise were crucial to the performance of wartime industrialists, but they profited enormously from government contracts, government subsidies and loans, and government tax breaks. Later they would profit from federal reconversion policy. Much more than in the 1930s, corporate leaders understood that the government and government spending could be their friend, not their foe. Big government and big business grew closer together, fundamental parts of the organizational society.

For organized labor the war brought important gains that were nonetheless more mixed than those for big business and left a more ambiguous legacy. Looked at from one perspective, the war years were years of great advances for labor. Union membership increased roughly from nine million to fifteen million workers, and by 1945 one-third of the nonfarm labor force was unionized—an historic high. The new Congress of Industrial Organizations (CIO), created in the 1930s, grew rapidly and substantially completed unionizing such crucial mass-production industries as automobiles, steel, and rubber. The percentage of workers covered by collective bargaining agreements rose from some 30 percent to 45 percent, and unions played a much larger role in American industry.

Unions also gained a more significant role in government agencies—the National War Labor Board (NWLB) and the War Manpower Commission (WMC) especially—and won important concessions from some of those agencies. The rapid growth of labor unions during the war came in large part from the 1942 NWLB "maintenance of membership" ruling, which held that workers not exercising an "escape period" option would be required to remain with the union until the end of the contract. A compromise between labor and employers, this both preserved an element of free choice and protected—indeed ultimately greatly enhanced—union membership.

Despite the lid it put on wage hikes with the 1942 Little Steel formula, the NWLB also found ways to help workers cope with rising living costs, by allowing such end runs around fixed wages as overtime pay and job upgrades. While hourly wages rose by about one-half from 1940 to 1945, weekly earnings increased by three-fourths. In decisions that prefigured the great postwar increases in benefit packages, the NWLB also allowed such hidden compensation increases as annual vacations and holiday pay, pensions, health insurance, and supplemental unemployment compensation.

Organized labor, then, could claim real gains from the war and an enhanced role in the organizational society. But there was another side to labor's status. A junior partner in the principal mobilization agencies, labor also was unable to achieve the role it wanted in the private sector. Whether at the national or plant level, union efforts toward joint labor-management direction of the war effort, even any significant union share of managerial authority, were fiercely resisted as an assault on the prerogatives of ownership. Those joint committees that existed rarely rose above the plant level and did little more than underwrite patriotic drives, stimulate greater worker effort, and address minor job-related difficulties. The largest firms in a number of key war industries would not allow the joint committees in their plants. Said General Motors president Charles E. Wilson, "As far as this equal-voice bunk is concerned, the answer is no."

Wartime strikes eroded the status and sometimes the power of organized labor. Despite real grievances and the fact that stoppages had no substantial impact on war production, wartime strikes damaged workers and unions in the eyes of most Americans and made them seem irresponsibly self-centered at best, dangerously unpatriotic at worst. One result was growing antiunion sentiment. Another was the Smith-Connally Act, which suggested that as compared to the 1930s business now had more to gain, unions more to lose, from government intervention in labor relations.

Finally, the war diminished the zeal and assertiveness of organized labor. In seeking to prevent or end many strikes, union leaders blunted the aggressiveness that had marked labor in the late 1930s and lost stature in the eyes of the most aggrieved or ideological workers and organizers. Beyond that, labor leaders, notably in the CIO, were generally more cautious and bureaucratic than they had been, and often less responsive to rank-and-file grievances. They were also more likely to stick to the basic bread-and-butter issues of wages, benefits, and conditions that employers would concede (and that workers typically cared most about) at the price of real power in national or industry policymaking. This attitude evidently also reflected the outlook of many new union members, especially newcomers to industrial work, who were concerned primarily with jobs, wages, and economic advance and often had no particular commitment to the union movement.

Agriculture's wartime gains and changes were less ambiguous than labor's though big farmers gained most. Like American business, indeed like most of the American people, farmers entered the war years with a version of "depression psychosis." For them the fear of glutted markets and ruinous prices that might follow a war boom grew not only from the experience of the depression decade but also from the boom-and-bust cycle of the World War I era. At first even a new war boom seemed chimerical; in 1939 and 1940 American agriculture, as it had been throughout the decade, was awash in surplus. Chester Davis, the defense commissioner for agriculture, proposed in November 1940 that five million low-income farm people should leave agriculture for defense industries.

But then demand increased, production and prices rose, and American agriculture entered an important—some thought revolutionary—period of expansion, prosperity, and change. On the home front, rising nonfarm employment and prosperity meant a much heavier demand for foodstuffs. Consumer spending on food rose from $14 billion in 1940 to $24 billion in 1944, and civilian per capita consumption of such items as dairy products, meat and poultry, and vegetables and grains all rose, quite different from patterns elsewhere in the world. But demand for American foodstuffs was buoyed not only by home-front consumers but also by the Allies and the armed forces. With Lend-Lease and the "Food for Freedom" effort, American farmers helped to supply the Allies in Britain, the Soviet Union, and China. The nation's farmers, like its industrialists and workers, played a key role in helping win the war.

Raising farm production by some 17 percent, the buoyant demand of the war years also more than doubled farm prices and income. Farm income rose from some $5.3 billion in 1939 to $13.6 billion in 1944, and on a per capita basis farm personal income almost tripled, outstripping the rate of increase for industrial workers. Farmers saw their assets appreciating in other ways as well, with the average value of farm acreage increasing by half and outstanding mortgage debt decreasing by one-fourth. Like urban Americans, farmers saved too, and deposits in rural banks increased dramatically. Although big farmers reaped the largest financial rewards, the war boom had a powerful impact on many small farmers as well.

World War II also reinforced major demographic and technological change in rural America. Between 1940 and 1945 more than 6 million people—almost 20 percent of the rural population—left the land for the armed forces and the defense industries in metropolitan areas. In all, the farm population fell from 30.5 million to 24.4 million during the war, from 24 to 18 percent of the nation's population; and the number of farms fell from 6.4 million to 5.9 million. The exodus was especially pronounced in the South and among farm laborers, sharecroppers, tenants, and marginal farmers. Many of the migrants had been unemployed or underemployed before the war, for while the farm population fell by some 6 million, agricultural employment fell by only 1 million.

Productivity gains enabled farm output to increase while agricultural employment declined. Almost half the increase in production came from higher yields. The war continued the application of technology and mechanization to American farms, a trend that favored especially the large commercial farmers. Part of the productivity increase came from greater application of fertilizers, disease and pest control, improved seed varieties, and better conservation, and part came from the much greater mechanization of American agriculture. Luck and good weather helped too, for wartime America escaped the dreadful droughts of the 1930s.

Changes in the farm sector led some agricultural historians

to label the war years the "second American agricultural revolution." Yet one should be wary about such a sweeping assess-
ment. The wartime decline in the number of farms, for
example, was comparable to that of 1935–1940 and 1945–1950,
and was significantly less than during the dramatic rural depopulation of the 1950s and 1960s. Tenantry and sharecrop-
ping had been on the decline before the war and continued
afterward. The increase in average farm size from 175 acres to
195 acres was roughly the same rate of increase as in the five
prewar years. Technological transformations in American
farming and the attendant growth of organized agribusiness
also both antedated and postdated the war. The war surely
continued and reinforced, sometimes accelerated, long-term
shifts and trends; but it did not by itself wrench American
agriculture into new patterns.

What the war certainly did, however, was to underwrite
prosperity, increase living standards, and raise expectations in
much of rural America. It did that not just for big commercial, mechanized farmers but for many small and marginal
farmers as well. Leslie Heiser, an upstate Illinois farmer, had
been embarrassed by his clothing and circumstances when he
was growing up; in 1947 his income allowed him to buy up-to-
date clothes as well as farm machinery and household appliances. "There isn't a job in New York City that's good enough
for me," he said.

Looking back on the war years, Laura Briggs, raised on a
small Idaho farm in the 1930s, recalled:

> Prior to the war we lived pretty much as people had since
> 1900. Farmers still relied heavily on horses. . . . In 1937 we
> finally got electricity and a refrigerator, but we had no in-
> door plumbing. . . . When I was growing up, it was very
> much depression times. . . . There was just no money any-
> where.

As farm prices [during the war] got better and better
... farm times became good times. Dad started having his
land improved, and of course we improved our home and
the outbuildings. We and most other farmers went from a
tarpaper shack to a new frame house with indoor plumb-
ing. Now we had an electric stove instead of a woodburn-
ing one, and running water at the sink where we could do
the dishes; and a hot water heater; and nice linoleum. . . . It
was just so modern we couldn't stand it. . . .

The war made many changes in our town. I think the
most important is that aspirations changed. People suddenly had the idea "Hey, I can reach that. I can have that. I
can do that. I could even send my kid to college if I wanted
to." These were things very few townspeople had thought
about before.

For Laura Briggs and her small-farm family, the war brought
prosperity, new status, a changed self-image, and rising aspirations. Although not universal, similar wartime experiences
were widely shared—in urban as well as in rural America.

A LEAVENING AGENT

The long-standing claim that World War II worked a
"many-sided social revolution" has included the idea that the
war was a sort of leveling agent, elevating the poor and disad-
vantaged and democratizing the nation's social structure. Certainly the war's impact felt revolutionary and liberating, then
and since, to many wartime Americans. But what people believe or remember is not always what happened; and what
happened to some did not necessarily happen to most.

One way to assess the war's impact on American society is
to examine data on income levels and distribution. Not surprisingly, the evidence is ambiguous. Figures on income gains
show that those toward the bottom of the socioeconomic scale

had much larger percentage increases than those toward the top:

PERCENTAGE INCREASE IN
AVERAGE FAMILY PERSONAL INCOME, 1941–1944

Lowest 20% of Families	96%
Second Lowest 20%	90
Middle 20%	72
Second Highest 20%	63
Highest 20%	53
Top 5%	41
Total Family Income	64

From another perspective, that of income distribution, there was a modest decrease in the shares of personal income for those at the top, a modest increase for those at the bottom:

PERCENTAGE DISTRIBUTION OF
AGGREGATE FAMILY PERSONAL INCOME

Income Group	1929	1935-36	1941	1944	1946	1950
Lowest 20%	12.5%*	4.1%	4.1%	4.9%	5.0%	4.8%
Second Lowest 20%		9.2	9.5	10.9	11.1	10.9
Middle 20%	13.8	14.1	15.3	16.2	16.0	16.1
Second Highest 20%	19.3	20.9	22.3	22.2	21.8	22.1
Highest 20%	54.4	51.7	48.8	45.8	46.1	46.1
Top 5%	30.0	26.5	24.0	20.7	21.3	21.4

*Lowest 40%

The 1941 to 1944 redistribution of income was comparable to what the depression had done from 1929 to 1935 and did not continue significantly after 1944. And the data on actual dollars earned provide still a different picture, in which the wealthy gained more and disparities widened:

AVERAGE FAMILY PERSONAL INCOME (CURRENT DOLLARS)

Income Group	1941	1944	1946
Lowest 20%	$ 450	$ 882	$ 982
Second Lowest 20%	1,044	1,979	2,178
Middle 20%	1,694	2,920	3,156
Second Highest 20%	2,463	4,014	4,290
Highest 20%	5,396	8,272	9,091
Highest 5%	10,617	14,963	16,796

Focusing on families in the highest 20 percent and the lowest 20 percent will help clarify what happened during the war. The income of the bottom 20 percent nearly doubled, rising 96 percent from 1941 to 1944, and its share of personal income increased from 4.1 percent to 4.9 percent of total income. By contrast, the top 20 percent saw its income increase by only half that rate, by 53 percent, and its share of personal income declined from 48.8 percent to 45.8 percent. Even so, the lowest 20 percent still earned less than 5 percent of all personal income while the highest 20 percent still earned more than nine times more, close to half of all personal income. The bottom 20 percent of families still earned on average well under $1,000 per year in 1944—a small sum indeed, even then. And the difference in dollars earned by the two groups actually *increased* by nearly 50 percent during the war, rising from $4,946 in 1941 to $7,390 in 1944. The war years thus saw modest *relative* income gains by lower-income (and middle-income) Americans but an *absolute* widening of income differences between them and the upper-income groups. And these data are only for income, not for total wealth, where large disparities were more entrenched. The war triggered neither a major nor an ongoing redistribution of income and wealth in the United States.

Still, the war clearly *seemed* a transforming event to many people, and there was reason for that. Jobs, even entry-level jobs at low wages, were better than unemployment. The average $882 that the bottom 20 percent of families earned in 1944 may not have been much, but it was nonetheless almost double what they had earned in 1941. (Corrected for inflation, their income increased by about three-fifths.) And even though the disparity in dollar income earned by rich and poor widened between 1941 and 1944, those at the bottom knew they had more income, higher living standards, and rising aspirations and expectations. If the war cannot fairly be called a leveling force, it seems to have been a powerful leavening agent: although the national income pie was sliced about the same way at the end of the war as before, each slice was bigger because the pie was so much larger. This was part of the appeal of Keynesianism in the 1940s and beyond to liberals and others who saw in economic growth a way dramatically to raise the living standards of low- and middle-income Americans without the politically difficult (and widely objectionable) purposeful redistribution of wealth and income.

But numbers and aggregate data tell only part of the story. The voices of wartime Americans both illuminate the numbers and go beyond them. Laura Briggs explained the impact of the war on many farm families; other Americans tell similar stories: "Going to work in the navy yard . . . , I felt like something had come down from heaven," recalled William Pefley, whose family had struggled during the depression and who moved from Pennsylvania to Portsmouth, Virginia. "It just made a different man out of me." Peggy Terry, a Kentucky woman who went to work in a shell-loading plant, said the income "was just an absolute miracle. . . . We had money and we had food on the table and the rent was paid. Which had never happened to us before." Roger Montgomery, who worked in an Ohio machine tool products plant, said that ". . . one of the important things that came out of World War

II was the arrival of the working class at a new status level in this society.... The war integrated into the mainstream a whole chunk of society that had been living on the edge." William Mulcahy said that "One of the major changes that the war brought about was a rise in hopes and expectations of young fellows like myself." Before the war he had worked in "a scrape-by job with very little to look forward to. The war allowed me to enter a whole new strata that I hadn't met before—middle management." It gave him and others "an opportunity for mobility and financial improvement."

If wartime work and income were transforming for many, so the armed forces and the GI Bill, with its educational benefits and its home, business, and farm loans, were for others. Before the war Larry Mantell, who served with the navy in the Pacific, "had no plans whatsoever to go to college. Financially it was just out of the question. But the GI Bill changed everything.... It was the war and going into the service ... that absolutely changed my life. I don't know what I would have been if it hadn't been for that." The GI Bill, said another man, "made us a far more democratic people."

Summarizing many assessments, James Covert, whose mother's small grocery store prospered during the war, concluded that World War II "changed our lifestyle and, more important, our outlook. You sensed that prosperity was coming. You started to think you could do things.... There was a feeling toward the end of the war that we were moving into a new age of prosperity."

For countless Americans across regional, occupational, class, ethnic, gender, and racial lines, the war was thus a leavening agent that changed individual lives. To be sure, the "depression psychosis," the fear of a return to the depression once the stimulus of war had ended, lingered on in wartime and postwar America, as did old and deeply entrenched disparities of income, wealth, status, and even opportunity. But the leavening influence of new circumstances, changed outlooks, and rising expectations had a real impact on wartime America and laid foundations for the economic boom and social change of the postwar era.

Helping to defeat the Axis, economic mobilization also vanquished the depression and began an extraordinary quarter-century of expansion and rising living standards, a period in which the American economy was the most productive and prosperous on earth. For big business, big farming, and even big labor, the war brought not only confirmation and reinforcement of their size and power but also greater public confidence in their ability to cooperate with government in producing full-employment prosperity and national power. Wartime economic mobilization produced dramatically new circumstances and new aspirations for the American people, demonstrated the capacity of the American economy, and brought jobs, money, pent-up purchasing power, and rising expectations that fueled postwar prosperity.

Some scholars have nonetheless suggested that wartime changes have been exaggerated not only in their extent but also in their beneficence. Even in the slack years of the late 1930s the American economy was the most productive on earth, and much of the economic growth after the war must be explained by postwar, not wartime, events. World War II neither began nor completed the evolution of the organizational society. The war boom was uneven—some regions, industries, groups, and individuals did far better than others—and economic mobilization often reinforced rather than reduced old disparities of wealth and power. Some economists would argue that "true" prosperity in a consumer-oriented market economy did not arrive until after the war.

Critics have further maintained that the growth in size and power of large organizations and interests came at the expense of economic and political democracy, that the organizational society harmed small enterprise and community autonomy. James Covert, the grocer's son who told of the galvanizing impact of the war on his family and its small business, also said: "Yet other changes were also taking place. . . . By the end of the war these Mom-and-Pop stores couldn't compete with the big supermarkets and the chain stores. People had cars and they began to go outside the neighborhood to shop. Society became larger, more impersonal. . . . By 1946 our little grocery store was gone. . . ."

Here too there is another side. The new supermarkets, for example, brought greater variety, lower prices, and sometimes higher quality than the old small stores. Mechanized agribusiness could often provide better, cheaper foodstuffs and other products. If the war helped workers more by way of jobs, wages, benefits, and working conditions than by enhancing labor's voice in national and plant policymaking, most seemed satisfied by the outcome. Nor did the large organizations that increasingly shaped and dominated American life bring only material advantages. The journalist-historian Nicholas Lemann has noted that Americans once "lived under the dominion of the standards of a town, or of an all-powerful boss, or of a parent, or of their local church." But by the post–World War II era, he says,

> . . . the power of these people and institutions had severely declined, and in their place large national organizations, operating strictly according to elaborate rules, had become more important. Instead of the town, there was a suburb whose merchants, architects, and employers were all huge national concerns. Instead of the boss, there was a corporation, or a federally funded university. These big institutions functioned less according to personal whim and more according to broad principles. So big institutions . . . meant more personal freedom, not less, as is commonly thought;

they meant the freedom that comes from not being under the rule of one person any longer.

Perhaps. But the essential point is that the impact of World War II was mixed and complicated, the nature of the wartime experience varied and sometimes ambiguous.

4

A Nation on the Move

WARTIME AMERICA was a nation on the move. Some sixteen million Americans joined the armed forces during World War II, and another fifteen million moved across county lines, eight million of them across state lines. In all, one in every five Americans made a significant geographic move during the war. Heading to war plants and military bases, migrants went especially to metropolitan areas and to the Sunbelt states of the Pacific, Gulf, and South Atlantic coasts, where war mobilization produced remarkable growth and change. Migration produced new experiences and new opportunities, reinforced a long-standing trend toward a more homogeneous national culture, and in a variety of other ways greatly influenced postwar economic, social, and political history. Demographic change involved population growth as well as geographic mobility, and increased marriage and birth rates helped set the stage for the baby boom and family culture of the postwar era.

Yet much of this was neither so new nor so beneficial as it sometimes seemed. Population redistribution—not only the movement to the Sunbelt but also rural depopulation and metropolitan and suburban growth—by and large followed patterns evident in the 1920s and 1930s. The marriage and birth rates of the war years were to a significant degree a return to the long-term trend interrupted by the depression. Wartime change, moreover, could be as disturbing as it was exhilarating. Uprooted from old patterns and communities, GIs and other wartime migrants often felt the shock and loneliness of dislocation. Feeling that their communities were being inundated with unwelcome newcomers who brought unwanted change, old-timers were often hostile to the migrants. Differences of race, class, and culture provoked tension and sometimes conflict. The war put added stress on families. Again, in short, the war's impact was complex.

GEOGRAPHIC MOBILITY

Americans hit the road and the rails in extraordinary numbers during the war, on the go to training camps, new jobs, new places. With automobile usage restricted by gasoline rationing, much of that travel was by train and bus. Indeed, for many wartime Americans a dominating memory of the war remained one of packed buses and trains, strained terminals, and keyed-up travelers seeking new destinations. Riding a crowded train to the West Coast and new opportunities, it occurred to one passenger that "it wouldn't take any imagination at all to think that you were going west on a covered wagon and were a pioneer again. It made me think of 'The Grapes of Wrath,' minus the poverty and hopelessness."

The contrast between the war years and the 1930s struck many observers, for wartime migration was fundamentally different in outlook and outcome. Expecting jobs and a better life, people left declining mining towns, ethnic and racial urban enclaves, depressed mountain areas, and struggling farms in the South and the Midwest for booming war communities where new opportunities beckoned. Some likened the influx of newcomers to wartime California to the gold rush of a century earlier. Migrants rarely struck it rich and sometimes struck out, at least at first; but most caught on somewhere, many got ahead in a way that had seemed impossible just a few years before, and some found their lives transformed.

But while the wartime migrations were different in character from those of the depression decade, and while they had major social, economic, and political consequences, the basic patterns of mobility and population redistribution largely continued those of past decades. The movement away from rural America, the influx to metropolitan areas and especially suburbs, the migration to the Pacific, the Gulf, and the South Atlantic coasts—these basic patterns of mobility were not new, indeed generally were much the same as in the 1920s and 1930s. And long-term forces, not just the impact of the war, explain why the population movement continued along the same paths once the war ended.

Still, even if wartime migration patterns were not new, they were striking and important. By one estimate twelve million people—nearly one of every ten—moved permanently to another state during the war. The farm population declined dramatically, by roughly one-fifth, as more than six million rural people left for the armed forces and for centers of defense production. Metropolitan areas, by contrast, expanded rapidly during the war, their populations growing by some 21 percent from 1940 to 1950, three times the rate of nonmetropolitan areas. Suburbs grew especially dramatically—by some 35 percent, while central cities grew by 13 percent—for suburbs had space available for new manufacturing plants, and space too for the new housing needed by war workers.

As millions of Americans headed to military installations and to new jobs in war production, they went especially to metropolitan areas on the Pacific, Gulf, and South Atlantic coasts, often to places that had shown the greatest population growth in the interwar decades. The combined population of

Oregon, Washington, and California grew by one-third from
1940 to 1945, while the national population increased by only 6
percent. West Coast cities grew especially fast, but inland
areas in the West attracted newcomers too.

Elsewhere population patterns were more complicated,
though again generally consistent with prewar trends. On balance the South lost population, as many rural folk went into
the armed forces or moved to defense production areas in the
North, Midwest, and West. But in metropolitan areas along
the Gulf and South Atlantic rim, from Corpus Christi and
Houston to New Orleans and Mobile, and then to Jack-
sonville, Charleston, and Norfolk, the population swelled dramatically, as it did in Washington, D.C. Large numbers of
migrants also went to such states as Michigan, Ohio, and Indiana, where established heavy industry converted to war production, and to Connecticut and parts of the Northeast where
metals, munitions, ship, and aircraft manufacture attracted
workers. But for the most part the nation's interior, especially
rural areas in the Midwest and South, lost population to the
coasts. And during the war, as before and after, the West and
parts of the South, especially the Sunbelt coastal areas, generally had significantly greater growth rates than did the Northeast and Midwest.

Like its destinations, the process and demography of
wartime migration also reflected long-term patterns. As in the
past, individual moves tended to be short range rather than
long range, with long-distance moves accomplished in "step-
ping-stone" fashion, by means of intermediary destinations
and jobs. As before, too, younger people were more inclined to
move than older ones, and migrants were typically in their
twenties or early thirties. Single people, especially young men,
were more likely to pick up and go, though family migration
became a feature of wartime life. Old constraints of gender

and race also shaped wartime population shifts. Women made up a large share of civilian migrants—ultimately some three of every five—but they typically moved as wives and daughters rather than as workers seeking opportunity. Because of persisting racial prejudice and discrimination, employers turned to black workers only as a last resort; the great tides of wartime African-American migration did not begin until 1943.

THE GROWING SUNBELT

The wartime experience of the Sunbelt states involved a telling combination of war-induced change and long-term continuities. No other part of the nation underwent such significant wartime growth as the South and the West, leading historians to use such terms as "watershed" and "great divide" to characterize the war's impact on these regions. Social and economic change came in part from government decisions to locate new plants in the South and West, not only because of available space and good weather but also out of a desire to stimulate economic growth and change in Sunbelt areas. Still, change was by no means the whole story of the wartime Sunbelt.

World War II had a dramatic impact upon the West. Barely more than 10 percent of the nation's population lived in the mountain states and on the Pacific Coast on the eve of the war. Manufacturing there accounted for less than 5 percent of the region's income and for less than 10 percent of national manufacturing—with much of that from California, which ranked eighth nationally in manufacturing in 1940. During the war the undeveloped and sparsely populated mountain states experienced substantial economic and population growth, but the great gains came in the three coastal states, California,

Oregon, and Washington. There striking economic growth and in-migration brought expansion, change, ebullience—and sometimes problems.

Economic mobilization was the catalyst. Continuing its traditional role in providing resources and programs essential to the development of the West, the federal government poured tens of billions of dollars into the region. In all, the government supplied some 90 percent of the region's new investment capital during the war. California alone received roughly 10 percent of all federal money spent during World War II. Shipbuilding, aircraft, and metals manufacture—steel, aluminum, and magnesium—needed for ships, planes, and other war goods led the way. From 1941 to 1945 Pacific coast shipyards and aircraft factories from Seattle to San Diego built about half of all ships and airplanes produced by the United States. Government funds created a new synthetic rubber industry and fueled growth in electronics. Defense-related science also developed rapidly—most spectacularly, of course, at Los Alamos, New Mexico, with the atomic bomb project, but also at the California Institute of Technology's Jet Propulsion Laboratory and elsewhere. Such developments put the West Coast at the forefront of the new aerospace industries and other defense-related wartime and postwar enterprises.

But federal money and its impact went beyond the defense industries. With its open spaces, good weather, and location facing the Pacific theater, the West was also the site of hundreds of military bases. Airfields, naval bases, army training camps, supply depots, testing areas, and the like were built with extraordinary speed and large impact in the coastal states and in parts of the mountain states and the Southwest. And military installations and in-migrant defense workers also triggered the growth of a variety of service industries throughout the region.

Some areas grew at spectacular rates. The population increased in San Diego County by more than 40 percent from 1940 to 1944, in the Portland-Vancouver area by about one-third, in the San Francisco Bay area by one-quarter, in the Puget Sound area by one-fifth. Those four areas together with Los Angeles were among the eight most congested wartime metropolitan areas according to the Census Bureau. Between 1940 and 1950 the U.S. population grew by 15 percent while the number of people increased by 22 percent in the mountain states and by 49 percent on the Pacific Coast. California grew by 53 percent, by more than 3.5 million people, in the decade, and nearly three-quarters of that growth came via in-migration.

The migrants largely came to stay, and many of the soldiers and sailors who had seen the Golden West during the war returned afterward. The area offered its newcomers visions of the good life, not only in jobs and rising living standards but also in a beguiling, even seductive style of living. Buoyed by the prospects and then the reality of jobs, the wartime migrants—predominantly young adults—lent a dynamism and an optimism to the West Coast that sustained and reinforced the war's impact. Economic and population growth expanded the West's role in virtually every aspect of American life in the postwar era.

Wartime migrations also produced a striking new heterogeneity in the region's population, particularly in the cities. The Hispanic population grew and moved increasingly toward the urban-industrial areas on the coast and to new occupational and educational opportunities as well as to traditional jobs in Western agriculture. Many American Indians departed their tribal lands, sometimes for the armed forces, more often for urban defense industries and new experiences in a way that triggered major change. And the Pacific Coast's African-American population soared once heavy black migration got under way after 1942. Defense jobs, rumors of the open, cosmopolitan West, and growing networks of friends and family ultimately attracted hundreds of thousands of African Americans, most from the deep South. Los Angeles experienced a particularly large black in-migration.

Yet the impact of World War II on California and the West should not be exaggerated. In economic as in population patterns, the war largely accelerated or confirmed developments long under way. The West, California especially, already had significant industrial capacity before the war; aircraft contracts went disproportionately to California, for example, largely because of the existing capacity of the state's aircraft industry, which in 1939 employed about half the nation's aircraft workers. Despite impressive numbers in wartime federal dollars, jobs, income, production, and the like, the relative national standing of California and the West, whether in absolute or per capita terms, changed little during the war—and often less than in parts of the old industrial heartland. A relatively minor industry both before and after the war, West Coast shipbuilding experienced only an ephemeral wartime boom. The spectacular 49 percent increase of the Pacific Coast population in the 1940s was almost identical to its 47 percent growth rate in the 1920s. Postwar population and economic growth, owing at least as much to long-term trends and the cold war as to World War II, often eclipsed wartime expansion. Certainly the West boomed during the war years, especially compared with the 1930s, but its growth was essentially continuous with long-term prewar and postwar trends.

The South experienced perhaps more fundamental, if less spectacular, change during the war. The historian Morton Sosna has suggested that World War II might have had a larger impact on the region than did the Civil War. For one thing, the war catalyzed a massive exodus from rural areas and a related reorganization of Southern agriculture. More than 3 million people—over one-fifth of the rural population—left the rural South during the war, many for the North and West. Ebbing a bit just after the war, migration picked up again in the 1950s; between 1940 and 1960 the rural South lost some 7.6 million people—more than half its population.

The depopulation of rural areas combined with other developments to bring major change to Southern agriculture. As late as 1940 Southern farming still depended upon staple crops produced by sharecroppers and small farmers relying on animal labor. During the war a mechanical revolution accelerated in Southern agriculture, crop and livestock diversification became more significant, and large, organized agribusiness increasingly dominated. The introduction of the mechanical cotton picker and other new devices together with the much greater use of tractors resulted in a continuing surplus of sharecroppers and tenant farmers that speeded migration from rural areas in the postwar years.

The economic results of this change were impressive. Between 1940 and 1944 Southern farm income catapulted from $2 billion to $4.7 billion, and per capita farm income soared from $150 to $454, not far off the national average of $530. In 1945 one in three Southern farms was electrified as against just one in six in 1939. Big farmers garnered the lion's share of the wartime boom, and while economic and political power in the hands of big farmers was scarcely novel in the South, the dimensions of wartime and postwar mechanized agribusiness were.

In other ways too the wartime boom spread its benefits unevenly across the South. While the region as a whole lost people to out-migration, cities, especially the coastal cities, grew rapidly. In all, thirty-nine of the forty-eight metropolitan areas in the South experienced rapid wartime population growth, and the Mobile, Norfolk, and Charleston areas accounted for three of the four most congested centers of wartime growth nationwide. Older inland cities like Birmingham and Atlanta also grew, but at nothing like the rate of the cities on the Gulf and South Atlantic coasts.

A boom city of another sort was Washington, D.C., where average income more than doubled during the war—the largest reported percentage increase in the country. From the dollar-a-year industrialists to the swarms of "government girls" who filled clerical positions, from admirals and generals to lobbyists and mid-level bureaucrats to black migrants looking for a chance, the population of the city swelled dramatically. Five thousand new government workers moved in each month during the peak growth, and the government grabbed or constructed hundreds of buildings. As David Brinkley has written:

> The war transformed not just the government. It transformed Washington itself. A languid Southern town with a pace so slow that much of it simply closed down for the summer grew almost overnight into a crowded, harried, almost frantic metropolis struggling desperately to assume the mantle of global power, moving haltingly and haphazardly and only partially successfully to change itself into the capital of the free world.

As with Washington, so with the rest of the South, federal money and defense mobilization lay behind wartime patterns of growth and change. Billions of dollars went south, partly in an effort to decentralize production and develop the South, called by FDR the nation's "number one" economic problem in the 1930s. The influence of powerful Southern Democrats in Washington also helped send money south. War Production Board chief Donald Nelson said that "A bird's-eye view of large-scale Southern industry makes you feel that the South has rubbed Aladdin's lamp."

Shipbuilding was the premier wartime industry along the coasts. The New Orleans–based Higgins enterprises were perhaps the most impressive, but Higgins was scarcely alone. Pascagoula, Mississippi, home of Ingalls Shipbuilding Corporation, went from a fishing town of a few thousand people to a war production center of thirty thousand. As the Alabama Dry Dock and Shipbuilding Company employed more than thirty thousand workers, once-stately Mobile became the nation's fastest-growing metropolitan area. With the Charleston and Norfolk areas on the Atlantic Coast also major shipbuilding centers, the South provided one-fourth of the ships built during the war.

Aircraft production soared too, particularly in the Dallas–Fort Worth and Atlanta-Marietta areas. Southern coal, iron, and steel production expanded, invigorating Kentucky and West Virginia mining and returning Birmingham steel production to full blast. More than half the nation's synthetic rubber was manufactured in the Gulf South, and the need for petroleum and petroleum products buoyed the Texas and Louisiana economies and laid the groundwork for more sophisticated petrochemical industries. Such older industries as cotton, tobacco, and textiles also profited from wartime demand. In all, industrial employment rose by 75 percent, from 1.6 million to 2.8 million.

Throughout the South, federal investment went into military bases as well as war production. With about one-fourth of the nation's population, the region received some 18 percent of federal war plant dollars—but some 36 percent of the money spent on military facilities. As the historian George B. Tindall aptly put it, the South "remained more campground than arsenal." Millions of soldiers and sailors passed through the South during the war, with large implications for regional, national, and personal history.

Thus World War II catalyzed industrial, agricultural, and population change in the South, often reinforcing developments already under way but accelerating their pace and im-

pact. And the tangible economic and social changes produced
intangible but important changes of outlook, aspiration, and
expectation that would also make the postwar South significantly different from the prewar South.

For one thing, migration and new jobs changed the circumstances and aspirations of countless Southerners. Moving from
dead-end work and poverty in the rural and small-town
South to new jobs and income in war production centers provided extraordinary new experiences. In such areas, migrants,
mostly young people, found not only jobs and money but
many of the trappings of modern life they had missed in the
countryside. "We'll have to have electricity to get tenants—
good tenants," noted a North Carolinian. "They won't come
otherwise; they want their electric refrigerator, radios, and
washing machines and all that."

For black Southerners, the wartime experience changed
outlooks and aspirations in still other ways. Many left the
South for the armed forces or for Northern and Western war production centers, never to return. But African-
American war workers and servicemen who did come back
often found Southern racial strictures and practices even more
oppressive and infuriating after having glimpsed the world
beyond and contributed to victory in the name of democracy.
To an important extent, the postwar civil rights movement in
the South was led by home-front and battlefront veterans who
had experienced different circumstances and a vision of change
during the war.

The war years laid groundwork for the postwar civil rights
struggles in other ways too. Many Northern servicemen,
white and black, who came south during the war left with a
new and different knowledge of Jim Crow, an antipathy toward the South, and a readiness to support civil rights efforts.
(Other whites moved south and adopted or acquiesced in
Southern mores.) A few Southern whites who left for the mil-

itary or defense jobs came back with a different and critical perspective on Southern attitudes and practices. For many other white Southerners, wartime developments and their implications, including new (though limited) federal efforts against discrimination and segregation, led to an increased resistance to civil rights campaigns and any challenge to the region's established racial patterns.

The South and West thus underwent visible and important change during the war. Each region experienced major economic growth because of wartime mobilization, and in different ways each saw patterns of social leavening and social change. Typically these confirmed or reinforced patterns and trends already under way, but they had profound implications not only for the two regions but for the postwar nation. Economic development and population growth in the Sunbelt came increasingly at the expense of the old "Snowbelt," or as it later came to be called, the "Rustbelt" of the northeastern quadrant. Reflecting shifting centers of populations, major league sports franchises would locate in the South and West, country music and evangelical religion became more important, Sunbelt lifestyles often set the nation's tone, and Sunbelt votes and political power increasingly supplanted those of the Northeast. From 1964 through 1992 every elected president was the resident of a Sunbelt state.

WARTIME COMMUNITIES

In the Sunbelt and elsewhere, rapid wartime change brought problems and conflict as well as new opportunities. To be sure, not all areas or communities experienced much stress. New York, a city of commerce and light industry, saw its size and rhythms affected relatively little by the war, while a host of smaller cities and towns across the nation felt the impact of war mobilization only indirectly. But the war-boom centers experienced the shock and challenge of rapid change, and old residents were often apprehensive about the alteration of their communities. The resulting issues were partly institutional and economic—how (or whether) to provide housing, schooling, and a variety of other costly services for the newcomers. But they were also social and cultural—how (or whether) to welcome newcomers who were strikingly different in background and behavior.

Migrants raised a number of concerns. Towns and suburbs feared that incoming workers would be black, or Catholic, or immigrant, and tip the ethnic and racial balance; that they would be loud or garish or backward or promiscuous and tip the social and cultural balance; that they would remain after the war and tip the balance toward decreased property values and increased welfare rolls and tax rates; that they would be Democrats (or Republicans) and tip the political balance. But two great lines of social division loomed above all others, one essentially class and cultural, the other racial.

In-migrants typically were working class, and while only a minority came directly from the farms, many did come from rural, mountain, and small-town America and carried with them obvious signs of their backgrounds. The taunts of "trailer trash" heard from Connecticut to California and from Mississippi to Michigan referred not so much to the mean lodging that the newcomers occupied as to their sociocultural status. Reflecting similar gradients of class and culture, established residents near growing military bases often disliked the dependents who tagged along, though officers' wives and families found a much readier welcome than did those of enlisted personnel.

Of the white in-migrants, poor folk from the South aroused particular distaste. Unused to the pace and demands of urban life, speaking and dressing differently, seemingly confused and even inept in trying to adjust to new and often hugely different circumstances, "hillbillies" and "briarhoppers" were targets of scorn and ridicule. Nearly a fourth of the migrants to the Detroit area came from Tennessee, Kentucky, Alabama, and Mississippi. Many Detroiters characterized the Southerner as "clannish, dirty, careless, gregarious in his living habits. He lives on biscuits and beans, never buys more than the most basic necessities of life, saves his money, is illiterate and yokelish." Indiana similarly received thousands of migrants from Appalachia, prompting the gibe (which had its Michigan counterpart) that the nation had lost three states: Kentucky and Tennessee had gone to Indiana, and Indiana had gone to hell.

But such antipathies were not confined to the North and were not simply a reflexive anti-Southernism. A Mobile schoolteacher said of the newcomers: "These are the lowest type of poor whites, these workers who are flocking in from the backwoods. They prefer to live in shacks and go barefoot, even when two or three workers in a single family earn as much as $500 a month. Give them a good house and they wouldn't know what to do with it....I only hope we can get rid of them after the war." And some did return home. "We found Detroit a cold city, a city without a heart or a soul," one David Crockett Lee said. "So we are going back to Tennessee...."

There were other sides to the story, and trouble and tension were far from the only themes. Many, likely most, Southern and rural migrants, especially the young and ambitious who dominated, adapted to new circumstances and new routines, learned how to manage vastly different lives and jobs, and carried their new experiences, skills, and outlooks and a new sense of the possibilities of American life into the postwar era. They also frequently encountered kindliness and help in adjusting. The churning and new encounters of wartime America, on the home front and in the armed forces, often diminished provincialism—whether of Southern hills and farms or Northern suburbs or urban ghettos—and bred a new, typically healthy sense of diversity and common cause. Old parochialism and prejudice ebbed as well as erupted.

Whatever the distaste, apprehension, and hostility that frequently met white newcomers, blacks provoked still more. For African Americans the war had a number of important and positive consequences, but it also exacerbated racial tension. In such war-boom cities as Detroit, Los Angeles, Mobile, and Norfolk (and in less frenetic cities too), racial conflict roiled wartime America, sometimes fomented by in-migrant Southern whites. Sybil Lewis, a young black woman who moved from segregated, small-town Oklahoma to Los Angeles during the war found "opportunities in California, but . . . a lot of prejudice and discrimination too. The Californians resented you coming in, getting good jobs. And the Southern whites who migrated to California were always dropping the 'nigger bit' to remind you they'd brought their prejudices with them." Aggravated by crowded conditions, dislocation, and wartime anxieties, racial prejudice was not confined to Southern whites.

Concern about in-migration and the associated resistance to change went beyond gulfs of class, culture, and race. Not just community character but community institutions were challenged. How to provide housing and schooling, police and fire protection, water and sewerage, recreation and medical care for the in-migrants pouring in? How to pay for such expansion? And what might happen to infrastructure and taxes when the war was over, especially if the newcomers departed? Many war-boom communities reacted like Hartford, Connecticut, "holding fast in a desperate effort to edge through the whole boom with the least possible local cost and the least possible expansion of facilities. . . . In this changing time Hartford does not want to change."

Housing was a particularly salient and significant issue, one involving federal policy as well as local response. From the beginning, war-boom communities could not cope with new housing needs. Trailer and tent camps sprang up, houses were subdivided and garages inhabited, families doubled and tripled up, and "hot bed" systems emerged where people slept as well as worked in shifts. Near Camp Polk, Louisiana, a reporter found young women and their children living in sheds, chicken coops, and barns, with "rooms" created by partitions and a separate area set aside for husbands and wives to have some semblance of privacy. Given the dimensions of the housing problem and its origins in national defense mobilization, towns and cities looked to Washington for help.

Help came, but it came slowly, partially, and in a way that reflected political and ideological battles of the war years. The Lanham Act of 1940 became the principal vehicle for federal help to war-boom areas, and in 1942 Roosevelt created the National Housing Agency (NHA) to consolidate and coordinate wartime housing programs. But housing lacked the priority given the military or industry, and never was sufficient for wartime needs. While liberals in Washington wanted carefully built, permanent structures that addressed long-term housing and slum-clearance needs, conservatives, joined by realtors, builders, and mortgage bankers, wanted temporary "demountable" structures that would not cost too much money, aggrandize government, or compete with the private housing market. Fearful of higher taxes, instant slums, depressed property values, and unwanted neighbors, the vocal middle class especially resisted government housing projects. The prospect that defense housing might attract blacks proved another barrier to adequate housing programs, and meant that defense housing often reinforced existing patterns of segregation—and sometimes created new ones—in North and South alike.

Eventually the government spent some $2.5 billion on new housing, and the NHA built more than 800,000 new units. Private construction—often with federally insured mortgage money—put up another million new units, and the worst of the housing deficit was met. Between underused existing structures and new construction, the NHA estimated that housing was found for seven million of the nine million migrants who needed it. But new wartime housing was predominantly temporary barracks, trailers, dormitories, and demountable structures. The combination of wartime migration, family formation and population growth, and temporary, inferior wartime housing bequeathed a huge housing problem to postwar America. Millions of new units needed to be built; millions of old ones were substandard.

If wartime communities were often reluctant to absorb new people and adopt new ways, mobility itself seemed to undermine community and stability. A mobile and transient society seemed more rootless, more impersonal, even more grasping than what many wartime Americans valued and remembered: "One of the biggest impacts the war had was to create a much more mobile society," said Don Johnson of Flint, Michigan. "As a result we have people who are not tied into the community structure in the same way they were before. They don't have the same sense of obligation to each other, or to the community. . . . Somehow, as a society, we have never gone back to the prewar values of family, friends, church and community."

But again the story was more complicated, often clouded by misperception and nostalgia, for America has always had a strikingly mobile society. In the long run the war did as much to create new communities and new ties as to disrupt or destroy old ones. Cooperating in bond and scrap-collection drives and civil defense efforts, celebrating local and national successes, lamenting setbacks and tragedies, griping about

shortages, rationing, and other problems—such common experiences and enterprises helped bring wartime Americans together. As migrants remained in their new communities and
proved themselves to be hard workers and good neighbors, as
newcomers and oldtimers alike learned more about each
other, differences faded, commonalities prevailed, and wartime tensions increasingly were left behind. Postwar migration continued community flux and national change.

FAMILIES AND CHILDREN

World War II had important consequences for American
families. Inaugurating a marriage and baby boom and reinforcing the emphasis on family life, the war also strained, disrupted, and sometimes destroyed marriages. Wives and
children often had to assume additional responsibilities and to
cope with loneliness and anxiety. Home-front children carried
their experiences, and sometimes their emotional scars,
through the rest of their lives. And a variety of wartime circumstances combined to make "latch-key" children, juvenile
delinquency, and sexual promiscuity sources of national concern.

The war brought striking growth in the marriage and birth
rates. Between 1939 and its wartime peak in 1942, the marriage rate jumped by more than 25 percent, and during the
war a larger proportion of men and women were married
than ever before. As marriages increased early in the war, so
too, predictably enough, did births. The birthrate rose by
more than 20 percent between 1939 and 1943 and then sky-
rocketed just after the war. Some demographers thus mark
the start of the baby boom era not with the 1946 explosion but
with the resurgence beginning in 1940.

Sensitive as always to economic conditions, the marriage
and birth rates of wartime America reversed depression-

decade patterns and reflected the buoyant attitudes produced
by war-induced economic recovery. But the prospects of separation also helped propel couples into marriage, as did the dislocation and loneliness of GIs and war workers far from home
and seeking comfort and security. Part of the increased
birthrate stemmed from "goodbye" babies conceived on the
eve of departure, products not only of last-minute and perhaps
careless lovemaking but also of a calculated desire to ensure a
next generation.

Mounting marriage and birth rates early in the war evidently also reflected in part another kind of calculation and
hedge against the future. It was widely expected that husbands and fathers would be deferred from the draft, and marriage rates increased sharply—by 50 percent in one
sixteen-state survey—when debate on conscription began in
the spring of 1940, and shot up again just after Pearl Harbor.
Similarly, the most noticeable early spikes in the birth rate
came in 1941, roughly nine months after the introduction and
after the passage of the Selective Service Act, and then again
ten months after Pearl Harbor and the American entry into
the war. It is impossible, of course, to assign weights to specific
reasons for the increased marriage and birth rates of the war
years. Affairs of the heart elude precise calculus, and, war or
not, this generation of Americans placed great value on family
life. But it is impossible to miss the multifaceted impact of the
war on family formation.

Entered into for a variety of reasons, often hastily, and
sometimes with little regard for the long term, many wartime
marriages had their problems. The absence of millions of husbands and fathers put strains, emotional and economic, on the
wives and children they left behind. Estimates vary, but the
number of households headed by a married woman with an
absent husband soared during the war; in June 1945 at least
four million husbands were away in the armed forces. Hun-

dreds of thousands of families moved across the nation, to military bases or defense production centers, in ways that put added pressures on family life. Some married couples grew apart during absences; some had never really been together or suited for each other; some saw wartime difficulties and changes—especially the new independence and autonomy of wives and the effects of battle on husbands—eat away the bonds of marriage. For some families the most traumatic wartime event was the return, not the departure, of the husband, for family members and family roles had changed. One consequence of this was the higher divorce rate of the war and early postwar years, which not only continued but reinforced and briefly accelerated a long-term increase in divorce. The divorce rate more than doubled between 1940 and 1946; by 1950 one million veterans had been divorced.

For all the strains and bad marriages, for all the difficulties of family life and childhood for millions of Americans, most wartime marriages turned out to be good and enduring, and the war probably helped to strengthen as many shaky marriages as it sundered. Children, like husbands and wives, had a variety of wartime experiences, often positive, that shaped their lives in big ways and small, consciously and unconsciously, in the years to follow. But those experiences were sometimes troubled too.

One home-front problem, partly real, partly exaggerated, was that of children left alone while the mother was at work and the father was at work or absent, usually in the military. Roughly one in five families was headed by a woman, for whom a job often was essential. Other wives and mothers also went to work, sometimes to supplement their husbands' wages or military allotment checks, sometimes to contribute to the war effort. But the number of working mothers has been exaggerated, as have the prevalence and difficulties of the latch-key children. Most families made large and usually

successful efforts to look after their children. The great up-
surge in working women came in the 14–19 and the 35–44 age
categories—typically women without children or with older
children. While the percentage of wives working outside the
home rose from 14 to 23 percent between 1940 and 1944, the
percentage of working mothers with children under six rose
only from 9 to 12 percent. (In 1990, by comparison, more than
half of women with children under age one were in the work
force.)

The emphasis on home and family also helps explain why
the day-care centers that might have helped children of working mothers were underfunded and underutilized. Under the
Lanham Act the federal government spent some $50 million
to help create roughly 3,000 day-care centers. But those centers enrolled only about 130,000 children and were in short
supply in the war-boom cities where they were most needed.
The inadequacy of the day-care centers reflected the reluctance of policymakers to fund such social projects and their
belief that the government should stay out of child care. Other
centers were provided by localities, churches, and some businesses (most notably Kaiser industries in the Pacific Northwest)—but they too typically were underused.

The underutilization of day-care centers stemmed partly
from such problems as distance, cost, transportation, and inadequate publicity. But many parents simply did not wish to
put their children in centers run by strangers and chose instead to make do in more traditional ways, especially by entrusting the care of their children to relatives, close friends,
or neighbors. Yet many child-care centers worked well, and
enrollments increased toward the end of the war. The Extended School Services program also helped care for children
of working parents. The numbers and problems of latch-key
children were often exaggerated by those who opposed wives

and mothers who worked, and wanted to trumpet the supposed awful consequences.

Still, some wartime children had real problems and real difficulties. Absent fathers, mothers doubly burdened by household duties and the need to earn money, the stress of migration and change, worry about loved ones and the war—all
these pressures and more took their toll on children on the
home front. Although serious maladjustment or misbehavior
characterized only a tiny minority of wartime children, truancy, juvenile delinquency, and promiscuity all gave cause for
concern. In Detroit the truancy rate jumped by one-fourth
during the war; in San Diego juvenile arrests in 1943 increased by 55 percent for boys, 355 percent for girls.

If the postwar concern about juvenile delinquency had
roots in wartime America, there is reason to doubt that it was
the national emergency often claimed. As in the case of day-
care centers, much of the adverse comment about juvenile
delinquency came from those concerned about changes in
family life and departures from old norms. For boys, a certain
rebelliousness and incidents of theft and mild violence were
the usual signs of distress. Most of it was minor and much of it
understandable in the flux and tension of the war years, with
the inevitable acting out of insecurity and adolescent pressure,
especially in a martial atmosphere with so many men away.
For girls, the wartime behavior most noted and most feared
was sexual promiscuity, or "sex delinquency" as it was sometimes termed. Here the symbol was the so-called "Victory
Girl" who frequented dance halls and bars and made herself
sexually available to servicemen. For many Americans the
Victory Girls represented the dangerous impact of the war on
old standards and traditional behavior and exemplified a general increase in sexual activity outside marriage.

In the long run the emergence of a self-conscious teen cul-

ture supported by high family and personal income may have
been a more important wartime development than juvenile
misbehavior. Both came not so much from parental neglect as
from the jobs, money, and time available to young people.
With many schools in war-boom areas going to double shifts
and with a variety of jobs available, young people had discre-
tionary spending power and a related autonomy that made
them a self-conscious and identifiable group, affected both by
peer pressure and attention from various agents of the consumer culture. As with so many other wartime patterns,
the growth of a discrete teen culture reinforced long-term
changes in social and economic patterns. In this area too, for
good and for ill, the war both continued prewar trends and
played a significant role in shaping and prefiguring important
postwar patterns.

The flux and mobility of wartime America brought
changes, challenged old ways and old preferences, and continued trends long under way. The nation was on the move in
many ways, yet neither the processes nor destinations were as
novel as they sometimes seemed. Changes in economic life
were welcomed and accommodated far more quickly than related challenges to social mores and standards. Cleavages of
class, culture, and race shaped action and reaction. Areas on
the new frontiers of change and growth—the Sunbelt states
most obviously, wartime Hawaii most intriguingly, with its
potent mixture of transiency, war tensions, multicultural ex-
change, and sexual and racial challenge—at once produced
significant change and provoked resistance and a determination to continue old ways. Many welcomed the new developments, many resisted them, most found in them a
combination of old and new, good and bad.

5

New Circumstances, Old Patterns

THE IDEA OF World War II as a fundamental and salutary divide in American history has especially characterized understandings of the war's impact on women and African Americans. For women, the enduring symbol is "Rosie the Riveter," the female industrial worker who signified the new circumstances and roles of wartime women that apparently led to postwar feminism and changing gender norms. For blacks, the March on Washington Movement of 1941 can represent how the war fueled protest, focused government attention, brought new opportunity, and laid essential groundwork for the postwar civil rights movement. Yet for both groups World War II also confirmed or reinforced trends long under way, and for both their wartime experiences were shaped and limited by old patterns and prejudices. The stories of women and African Americans— together more than half the nation's population—thus provide particularly useful perspectives on the notions of World War II as a watershed and as the Good War.

WOMEN AND THE WAR

The image of Rosie the Riveter has powerfully framed interpretations of the impact of World War II on women and gender roles, but the image is misleading. Most women were not regularly in the workforce; most women workers did not have industrial jobs; the great majority of wives did not work outside the home; and women's roles reflected important continuities as well as the war's impact.

The question of women in the workforce has dominated much of the discussion of women and World War II, partly because of wartime change, partly because economic roles are so intertwined with other fundamental social patterns and processes. Three developments especially marked the female labor force during the war: the number of women in the workforce grew dramatically; women were distributed differently among the various occupational categories; and older and married women took jobs in especially large numbers.

Most of the wartime growth and change in women's employment came after 1942. At first employers looked chiefly to hiring men, and some women quit their jobs and returned home as their husbands gained employment or took better jobs. Federal agencies initially counseled against recruiting women until men were employed, and then typically discouraged hiring mothers of young children. As labor needs increased, government and industry launched vigorous but only partly successful campaigns to attract women workers. The wartime expansion of the women's labor force thus came slowly and often grudgingly, but the mid-war years saw great expansion and change. Women worked for patriotic reasons, for adventure, for personal advancement, and often for essential income—because they were single or because their husbands, including low-paid GIs who could send home only small allotments, did not earn enough.

During the war the number of employed women shot up by about 50 percent, roughly from twelve million to eighteen million, as women provided one-third of the additional workers needed for the wartime labor force. Between 1940 and

1945 the proportion of women employed grew from 28 to 37 percent, and by 1945 women formed 36 percent of the civilian labor force as compared with 26 percent in 1940. These numbers actually understate the extent of women workers, for women continued to be more likely than men to enter and leave the labor force, especially in order to attend to family responsibilities. Thus in 1944, for example, on average some 37 percent of adult women were in the labor force during a given week, but 48 percent worked at some point during the year.

At least as important as the growth of the women's workforce were changes in the profiles of women's jobs and women workers. In the sex-segmented work force of 1940, roughly three in ten women workers were clerical and sales workers, and another three in ten were service workers; about two in ten were industrial workers. Women accounted for 2 percent of skilled workers and foremen, 12 percent of managerial workers, 26 percent of factory operatives, 28 percent of sales workers, 53 percent of clerical workers, and 94 percent of domestic service workers.

The most noted wartime changes in the women's workforce came in defense industries, where women took production jobs as riveters, welders, and an array of other positions previously confined to men. Some 1.7 million women worked in steel, machinery, shipbuilding, aircraft, and automobile factories in 1944 as against 230,000 before the war. Women were 26 percent of factory operatives in 1940, 38 percent in 1945. By 1944 there were 2.5 million more women blue-collar workers than in 1940, up to nearly one-third of the female labor force.

The circumstances of wartime industrial employment nonetheless reflected old norms. Recruitment drives stressed that women were replacing men only "for the duration" of the war and took pains to reassure men and women alike that women would remain feminine despite their new jobs. Sometimes the jobs were described in traditional domestic terms—

women might adapt to factory jobs "as easily as to electric cake-mixers and vacuum cleaners." And women were expected to work in women's roles in another sense—as wives, mothers, and sweethearts supporting their men in the armed forces. On the job, women found other signs of old attitudes. Men often responded with hostility or condescension (though others helped or came to respect women workers), and women's sexuality was often emphasized by men and by factory newspapers or magazines in ways that discomfited many women and seemed to demean them and their work.

Old constraints as well as old stereotypes persisted. Women in the industrial labor force were largely confined to work as helpers, record-keepers, and semiskilled laborers, with jobs as riveters and welders marking more the ceiling than the floor. From 1940 to 1945 women's percentage in the category of craftsmen, foremen, and skilled workers rose only from 2.1 to 4.4 percent—and then fell back to 2.1 percent by 1947. In 1942 the National War Labor Board declared that women should receive equal pay for "work of the same quality and quantity," but despite some progress the ruling was often ignored or circumvented. Labor unions, though admitting women, typically did little to combat job and pay discrimination, to improve women's status, or to protect women's jobs. Reflecting not only discrimination in wage rates but also women's greater concentration in lower-paying jobs and industries, their relative lack of experience and seniority, and their tendency to have more part-time and less overtime work, the average weekly wage of women manufacturing workers in 1944 was $31, that of men $55.

Women faced special burdens as well. Only slowly did employers improve facilities and working conditions for women, or did communities provide day-care centers or alter store hours so that working women could shop for themselves and their families. Many husbands disapproved of their wives working, and most did little to share burdens at home. Working women thus typically worked a "double day," with long hours of family chores after their factory or office jobs, and domestic work that was often more arduous than before because of various wartime shortages and inconveniences. Together with unpleasant working conditions, the demands of the double day help to explain women's higher rates of absenteeism, turnover, and part-time work.

Despite these limits and difficulties, the wartime experience was important. Not only did women work in new and different jobs and earn needed money, but as they persevered and succeeded they gained self-confidence and self-knowledge they would carry the rest of their lives. Adele Erenberg, an aircraft worker during the war, recalled that "For me defense work was the beginning of my emancipation as a woman. For the first time in my life I found out that I could do something with my hands besides bake a pie. . . . I had the consciousness-raising experience of being the only woman in this machine shop and having the mantle of challenge laid down by the men, which stimulated my competitiveness and forced me to prove myself."

Wartime developments in the white-collar sector were perhaps even more significant for women than those in industry, for they were more permanent and more consistent with long-term trends. Between 1940 and 1944 the number of women office workers increased by some two million, from about one-fifth to one-quarter of the female labor force, and did not decline as rapidly as blue-collar jobs at war's end. The federal government provided much of the new white-collar opportunity, for the number of women civil service workers soared from less than 200,000 in 1939 to more than one million in 1944, and from 19 to 38 percent of federal workers. In all, between 1940 and 1950 the number of women in white-collar jobs increased by 53 percent while the number of women in all

other categories grew by just 13 percent. Clerical and secretar-
ial work became more a "feminine domain." Most women
preferred white-collar work, which seemed more fitting and
more likely to enhance their status and security. And for
white-collar as well as for blue-collar women workers, the
wartime experience mattered. Inez Sauer, a thirty-one-year-
old housewife with two children, took a job as a clerk with
Boeing Aircraft despite objections by her parents and husband. At Boeing, she said, "I found a freedom and an independence I had never known. After the war I could never go
back" to being a housewife and club woman. "The war
changed my life completely."

The war brought major structural change in white-collar
work as well. It was during the war, for example, that women
gained a substantial foothold in such jobs as grocery clerks
and bank tellers, while in banking and other professions
women began to move in significantly larger numbers into
middle management. Perhaps even more important was the
related rapid decline of the "marriage bars" that had for
decades kept married women from a range of white-collar
jobs in business and government. Implemented originally because of evidence and expectations that married women were
likely to leave the work force, and then reinforced by depres-
sion-era concerns about sharing jobs equitably among families, marriage bars were ignored or dropped—permanently
for the most part—when wartime labor recruitment drives
turned increasingly to married women.

Changes came also in the demographic composition of the
female labor force. Three-fourths of the new women workers
were married, and three-fifths were over thirty-five years old.
With roughly one of every ten wives entering the labor force,
the percentage of wives in the work force rose from 14 percent
in 1940 to 23 percent in 1944. Participation rates of women
aged 35 to 44 increased from 27 to 37 percent. By war's end

there were, for the first time, more married than unmarried women workers, and more over than under thirty-five. Persisting in the postwar era, these were changes of large importance—though they owed at least as much to long-term economic, social, and demographic forces as to the impact of the war.

Racial characteristics of the female work force changed too. From 1940 to 1944 the number of black women workers rose by over a third, from 1.5 to 2.1 million, and the percentage working increased from about 33 to 40 percent. (Because white women entered the work force in much larger numbers, the black share of the female labor force fell from 13.8 to 12.5 percent.) The proportion of African-American women working as domestics fell from 57 to 44 percent, the percentage working in agriculture from 21 to 11 percent. By contrast the percentage of black women in industrial jobs rose from 6 to 18 percent, and the percentage in commercial service (cleaning, cooking, serving, and the like in offices, hotels, and restaurants) increased from 10 to 19 percent.

But such changes came with old limits. Outside the federal government, few black women were hired as clerks and secretaries, and almost none found employment as saleswomen except in the relatively few black enterprises. In industry, African-American women were generally hired in the least appealing and poorest-paying jobs. Racial discrimination —and its legacy in lower levels of education and experience— was clearly the major factor in the much different occupational patterns of black and white women. Black women could find greater opportunity in defense plants in the North and West, but barriers and disparities of race in training, hiring, and promotion existed throughout the country.

Another important and revealing aspect of women's wartime experience came in the military, where for the first time women achieved regular status and were used in almost every capacity except combat. As in industry, change came slowly, limited by both male chauvinism and male chivalry. But the fact that a large share of duties in the modern armed forces was essentially administrative and clerical persuaded military leaders to include women—and thus free more men to fight. By mid-1942 the navy accepted women into the WAVES (Women Accepted for Volunteer Emergency Service) on the same basis as male reservists, and a year later the larger WAAC (Women's Army Auxiliary Corps) achieved full military status as the WAC (Women's Army Corps). Ultimately more than one-third of a million women entered the uniformed forces during the war.

Never more than 2 percent of the armed forces, women faced a variety of constraints. Wives were discouraged from service; women with children under fourteen (the WAC) or eighteen (the WAVES) could not enlist; servicewomen were not automatically granted dependency allowances for spouses or children; women officers were not to give orders to men; and black women encountered quotas and racial prejudice. Not including nurses, nearly four-fifths of the Wacs served in clerical positions; unlike Germany and the Allies, the United States explicitly forbade women from combat duties or positions with units that had a combat mission. Roughly a thousand women served as Women's Airforce Service Pilots (WASP) and flew a variety of military aircraft in Canada and the United States, ferrying planes, towing targets, and even serving as test pilots; but they never achieved full military status, and Congress terminated the program in 1944 when the women were no longer needed. Only nurses, who had traditions of service and of professional status and who did not threaten established gender norms, found ready acceptance and real opportunity in the armed forces; and only they saw any significant service in the war theaters.

Male GIs typically were unhappy about women in the military, and much of the public was dubious. Condescension and hostility toward what the press sometimes called the "Petticoat Army" characterized many responses. Rumors were spread about the promiscuity—whether heterosexual or homosexual—of female soldiers and sailors, stories that demoralized women and depressed enlistments. Some men, and their mothers, wives, and sweethearts too, were unhappy about an early reason given in recruiting servicewomen—to "release a man for combat." But despite such reactions, women in the military constituted a significant new departure and changed some minds about what women should and could do.

More traditional was the enlistment of women in a variety of home-front volunteer and service endeavors. Whether participating in scrap and bond drives, or working with such federal agencies as the Office of Price Administration, or helping the Red Cross and the United Services Organization (USO, which provided recreational centers and activities for GIs), millions of women—perhaps one of four, though especially middle-class white women without young children—served as home-front volunteers in the war effort.

But the principal and overwhelmingly preferred wartime role of American women was that of wife and homemaker. Indeed, World War II may well have had a larger impact in promoting natalism and the primacy of family than in expanding employment and the public roles of women. Although wartime needs and the performance of women in a variety of jobs altered attitudes to some degree, opinion surveys throughout the war revealed that a large majority of men, and of women too, believed that women, wives especially, belonged at home. Asked to choose their ideal life, three-fourths of young women surveyed in 1943 preferred being a housewife, 7 percent preferred being single with a successful career, and 19 percent hoped to combine marriage and a career. Asked to decide between the two, just 20 percent of the last group preferred a career to marriage. Most housewives thought their best contribution to the war effort was in the home.

Behavior followed attitudes. Seven of eight women at home in 1941 remained there in 1944, despite production needs and recruitment efforts. Of the twelve million working women of 1941, two million—one of every six—by 1944 had left the labor force to return home. Of wives with husbands at home in 1944, three-fourths had been homemakers since 1941; about 11 percent were working in both 1941 and 1944; and 5 percent had quit and 8 percent had entered the labor force since 1941. Women with absent husbands, in particular GIs' wives, worked in significantly higher proportions, though fewer than one of ten wives saw their husbands leave for the military. Women with children under six had the lowest working rate, rising from just 9 to 12 percent during the war.

This focus on family and domesticity also appeared in the rising marriage and birth rates of the war and postwar years. By the late 1940s marriage rates evidently were higher, the average age of first marriage lower, and proportionately more women were married than ever before in the nation's history. Increases in marriage and fertility rates were highest among young, educated, urban women. The ideal family size rose from two to three children in the 1940s, and reality marched toward the ideal.

But history, as ever, was complicated. Despite wartime preferences for domesticity and the reluctance of many women to enter the labor force, polls toward the end of the war showed that most working women—typically two-thirds or more, including half or more of married women—wished to remain at work, often at the same jobs, after the war. Government and business, however, now urged them to return home as the war wound down. Many women thus lost their wartime positions, typically replaced by men, and neither servicewomen nor women defense workers received the same sympathy or help as male veterans and displaced war workers.

Women remained a regular part of the postwar military, and polls showed that a small but clear majority of the American people favored women in the armed forces. Impressed by the performance of women in the war, military leaders believed they would continue to play important roles, especially in clerical and hospital work. But demobilization reduced the number of women in the services from 266,000 to 14,000, and women were limited to 2 percent of the postwar armed forces, faced restricted advancement opportunities, could not enlist if they were married unless they had served previously, and were placed in occupations deemed acceptable for women.

War's end also brought substantial cutbacks of civilian women workers, at rates much higher than those for men, and a channeling back to traditional jobs. In the automobile industry, which had converted to military production during the war, the percentage of women fell from a wartime high of some 25 percent to just 8 percent by 1946; similar patterns obtained in shipbuilding, aircraft, and other defense industries. About one million women had left factory jobs by early 1947. In such areas as light industry and white-collar and service employment, by contrast, women's employment held steady or even rose. In all, the percentage of women in the workforce fell from 37 to 30 percent between 1945 and 1947, and women's share of the workforce fell from 36 to 28 percent. Roughly one-third of the women—and about half the married women—who entered the labor force during the war had left it by 1950. Reflecting movement toward lower-paying jobs as well as shorter working hours and less seniority, women's average earnings fell sharply, and the gap between men and women's earnings widened.

A variety of forces and factors, not always easy to interpret,

lay behind these early postwar patterns. Seniority rules and
veterans' preferences led to widespread layoffs among women
factory workers, as did continuing fears of postwar unemployment and a widespread sense that women should return home
and leave the jobs for men. Many women who "quit" thus did
so because they saw no alternative. On the other hand, many
who were "laid off" would have left wartime jobs anyway for
other employment or for the home. And though husbands'
preferences and social pressures counted heavily in many
women's decisions, so too did their own desire to return home.
Large majorities of housewives polled in the postwar years
thought it no sacrifice to leave work for home and thought
their family came first.

But many women still wanted to work and for financial
reasons needed to work. After declining in the first year or so
after the war, women's employment began to rise again by
1947, especially in white-collar and lighter blue-collar work.
During the 1940s the percentage of married couples who both
worked doubled, from 11 to 22 percent. By 1950 more women
were working than in 1944, and women were some 30 percent
of the labor force—up from the 26 percent of 1940 and about
in line with the long-term trend. Among white married
women employed in 1950, only about one in five had joined
the labor force during the war; more than half had been employed in 1940; and the rest had taken jobs after the war.
Clearly the expanding and changing postwar economy, inflation, rising material aspirations, and other long-term prewar
and postwar developments, not just the war, lay behind the increasing workforce participation by women.

World War II also had implications for the education, legal
status, and political roles of American women. High school
completion rates increased for women in the 1940s and out-
stripped men's, though beyond high school, and especially in
postgraduate training, women continued to lag well behind.

The war brought some advances in legal status—fewer proscriptions against jury duty, for example, and renewed efforts for equal pay and an equal-rights amendment—and brought more women into public service and politics and more attention to women's issues. In such ways, however, the war generally reinforced long-term developments.

So too the war evidently had relatively little impact on long-range growth and change in the women's workforce. Especially because of increasing high school graduation rates for women, the rapid growth of white-collar sales and clerical employment, rising living standards and expectations, and the growing twentieth-century preference for wives rather than children supplementing the husband's income, women had been entering the workforce, especially the white-collar workforce, in larger numbers for decades. The war reinforced and accelerated that pattern, and it briefly led to a higher concentration of women in more physically arduous blue-collar jobs. After the war long-term patterns reasserted themselves.

But those patterns were also altered by new wartime circumstances. The lowering of marriage bars against women in white-collar jobs turned out to be particularly important. In the postwar era, as so many young women devoted themselves to family and children, employers turned increasingly to older married women who could, and did, take jobs in the rapidly expanding white-collar universe. Marriage bars thus stayed down, and white-collar and middle-management jobs remained significantly more available to women. Ironically, then, postwar feminism and changes in gender roles and norms stemmed in part from the increased focus on family and motherhood of young women in wartime and postwar America.

The dynamics of home and family sometimes changed too. Especially when husbands were away, the household became a place for greater responsibility and autonomy for women as they coped with the difficulties of wartime life. In younger and white-collar families most notably, households often became more egalitarian, and not only when the wife worked outside the home. Sometimes marriages also became more troubled as women sought to continue new roles and responsibilities while husbands preferred to return to old ways. Long-term trends figured in this, of course, but so too did the wartime experience.

Finally, the war also accelerated the understanding among women, and evidently among many men, that women's capacities were broader and deeper than old definitions of "women's work" and "women's place" would have permitted. Harder to see or measure than labor force participation rates, occupational structure, and the like, such individual experiences and perceptions were also a crucial part of the war's impact. In 1942 Charlcia Neuman got her first job at age thirty-two at Vultee Aircraft in California. Her husband acquiesced only because the family needed the money, and she was happy to leave the labor force when she was laid off in September 1945. But she later concluded that wartime work "was a very good experience for me because of the challenge of doing something like that, to prove to myself that I could do it." And "I always felt that if married women needed to work, then that was their choice. I felt with my own daughter that if she wanted to work, she should be trained to do something where she would be paid good money. . . ." Her daughter became a college-educated career woman. If there was little overt feminism among wartime women, during or after the war, and much evidence of a focus on family and of long-term employment trends only partly affected by the war, World War II nonetheless had an important impact on millions of American women, on gender roles and norms, and, in sundry and sometimes indirect ways, on the emergence of postwar feminism.

AFRICAN AMERICANS AND THE WAR

The circumstances of African Americans generally were dismal on the eve of World War II. The black unemployment rate in 1940 approached twice the white rate, and black median family income was barely more than one-third that of whites. Five percent of African-American males held white-collar jobs as against one-third of whites, while two-thirds of black workers but only one-fifth of whites were in service or unskilled jobs. Three-fourths of employed black women worked as domestic servants or agricultural workers. One in ten black adults had no schooling, and the median level of education was two-thirds that of whites. African-American mortality was much higher, life expectancy significantly lower. Black housing was typically segregated, inferior, and overcrowded.

Such patterns partly reflected the fact that three of four African Americans lived in the South, where the Jim Crow system left blacks segregated by law, vulnerable to white prejudice and violence, and largely disfranchised. But whether North or South, urban or rural, African Americans found themselves in a racial caste system that affected virtually every aspect of their lives. The depression decade had brought them new attention from the federal government and had seen important instances of organized black protest and community action, but little had been done to ameliorate the conditions of African-American life.

Prejudice and discrimination also shaped the national defense buildup of 1939–1941. Of 100,000 aircraft workers in 1940, for example, only 240 were black—and most of them janitors. North American Aviation spoke for many other aircraft and defense firms in explaining that "The Negro will be considered only as janitors and in other similar capacities.

Regardless of their training as aircraft workers, we will not employ them." The United States Employment Service honored "white only" requests from defense industries, and the early mobilization agencies similarly acquiesced in such practices and in placing blacks in "traditional" jobs.

Denied opportunity in the expanding defense industries, African Americans also encountered discrimination and segregation in the armed forces. At the outset of the war neither the Marine Corps nor the Army Air Corps would accept blacks; the navy allowed them to enlist only as cooks and stewards; and the army accepted limited numbers, typically placed them in all-black units, and trained them for noncombatant roles. Like other army officials believing that blacks should not be entrusted with demanding jobs or leadership positions, army Chief of Staff General George C. Marshall said that desegregation would harm the morale and efficiency of the fighting forces by departing from patterns "established by the American people through custom and habit."

From the start, this exclusion from defense and military opportunities stung African Americans and stirred protest. Remembering the failure of the World War I "close-ranks" strategy—of forgoing protest during the war in order to bring anticipated gains for loyalty and service—black leaders intended this time to protest as well as participate. The wartime "Double V" slogan of black organizations and newspapers symbolized the conscious intent of many African Americans to fight for their own "double victory"—"victory over our enemies at home and victory over our enemies on the battlefields abroad."

Begun well before Pearl Harbor, efforts toward change in the armed forces and defense industries yielded some early results. The army began in late 1940 to accept larger numbers of blacks, proportional to their share of the population, to introduce blacks into the Army Air Corps, and to provide training as officers and combat soldiers. Colonel Benjamin O. Davis was promoted to brigadier general, the first African American to hold such a rank, and black advisers were assigned to the secretary of war and the Selective Service director. Although limited, these steps marked the beginning of wartime change that would lead to the substantial desegregation of the armed forces by the 1950s.

The question of military service had special emotional and symbolic value, but black leaders and organizations also pressed hard in 1940 and 1941 for action on jobs. When early efforts proved largely fruitless, the charismatic black leader A. Philip Randolph, head of the Brotherhood of Sleeping Car Porters, the leading black union, formed the Negro March on Washington Committee and in January 1941 declared that it would organize a massive march on Washington, D.C., under the slogan: "We loyal Negro American citizens demand the right to work and fight for our country." The March on Washington Movement (MOWM) differed from other similar efforts in that it was an avowedly all-black attempt to mobilize the masses of African Americans toward direct action and was concerned not so much with the South and legal rights as with the circumstances and economic opportunities of all African Americans, North as well as South. Pathbreaking in important ways, the MOWM also turned out to be surprisingly successful, a milestone in American history.

Meeting with President Roosevelt on June 18, 1941, Randolph presented a list of demands, including an end to discrimination in training and employment and an end to discrimination and segregation in the government and in the armed forces. Roosevelt was not unsympathetic to the plight of black Americans, and throughout the war he was urged to do more on civil rights and other areas of social reform by his wife, Eleanor Roosevelt. But the president consistently placed domestic reform, including civil rights, secondary to the pri-

mary aim of defeating the Axis. Wary of riling Southern
Democrats, he also feared national embarrassment should the
march take place, especially if it provoked violence in the nation's capital. FDR thus tried various forms of vague reassur-
ance, pressure, and suasion to head off the march, but
Randolph demanded more; he required "something concrete,
something tangible . . . and affirmative."

On June 25 Roosevelt signed Executive Order 8802. Barring "discrimination in the employment of workers in defense
industries or Government because of race, creed, color or national origin," it ordered an end to discrimination by government agencies, job training programs, and defense contractors
and established a Fair Employment Practices Committee
(FEPC) to investigate complaints and implement the executive order. For the first time FDR had taken major public action on behalf of civil rights; indeed, for the first time since
Reconstruction the federal government had created an agency
committed to action toward equal rights for African Americans. While the executive order did not include the armed
forces and did not address segregation, it was a signal victory
for Randolph and the MOWM.

Despite the initiatives of 1940 and 1941, and the continued
prodding of civil rights advocates, wartime gains came slowly.
Discrimination, segregation, and sometimes exclusion, including separate training facilities and assignment to service and
noncombat units, marked the various branches of the military
for much of the war. Whites commanded black combat units;
black officers typically were assigned to noncombat units; and
no black officer assigned to a unit could outrank a white officer. Black GIs experienced racist treatment at the hands of
many commissioned and noncommissioned white officers,
and often encountered still worse treatment off base, particularly in the South where much training was conducted.

But there was another side. More than a million African

Americans served in the military, and despite segregation and discrimination the armed forces provided training, experience, and new perspectives that lifted the horizons and aspirations of black GIs and often launched them on new career paths. For many, their wartime experiences also contributed to a sense that they must work all the harder for victory at home once victory abroad had been achieved. Those who got to England or France or Hawaii and experienced fairer and more friendly treatment came back with a new sense of the possibilities of race relations. As one black veteran said upon returning home from the Pacific, "*Our* fight for freedom begins when we get to San Francisco."

Change did occur. In April 1942 the navy agreed to accept African Americans for general service, and by the fall of 1944 some five hundred black sailors were serving in such capacities as radiomen and gunner's mates in integrated crews on twenty-five ships. All restrictions on assignments for blacks in the navy were ended in 1947, partly because analysis showed that integration yielded more combat efficiency than segregation. The Marine Corps accepted blacks for the first time during the war, and the Army Air Corps provided combat opportunity for African-American pilots and crews. In 1944 the army began to desegregate training camps, though local opposition in the South often thwarted the efforts; and by the winter of 1944–1945 black combat troops were serving with distinction in Europe, and some volunteers began to integrate formerly all-white units during the desperate days of the Battle of the Bulge. Aviators in the black 99th Pursuit Squadron compiled a distinguished record of valor and effectiveness. The army's Gillem Report, released in 1946, indicated that efficiency and equity alike pointed toward full and unfettered participation. Although the army was criticized by civil rights groups for timidity in implementing the ideas of the report, it was nonetheless another important sign of the war's impact.

Despite the special significance of the military, changes in black occupational and geographic distribution had perhaps even more profound long-term consequences. At first neither the burgeoning war economy nor the Fair Employment Practices Committee seemed to have much impact on black employment patterns. Successful in only about one-third of the cases brought to it, the FEPC lacked sufficient money, staff, support, and power and often seemed too ready to accommodate to public opinion. Its only real authority was to recommend terminating contracts to offending firms—a hollow threat, for the administration would not cut off production essential to the war effort.

The FEPC did have its successes, and in its day-to-day activities kept pressure on employers and unions, worked to ensure that blacks were not just hired but were employed at levels commensurate with skills and training, and provided its staff experience and contacts that later proved useful in the postwar civil rights movement. Nor did the FEPC provide the only institutional evidence of change: the National War Labor Board prohibited race-based wage differentials, the U.S. Employment Service stopped acceding to "white-only" labor requests, and the National Labor Relations Board declared that it would not certify unions that excluded minority groups. Even so, it is hard to escape the conclusion that, as for women so for blacks, it was the necessities of war, in particular the mounting labor shortage, more than principle and public policy that brought employment gains.

For whatever combination of reasons, economic advances for blacks did come from 1943 on, especially in the North and West. African Americans won not only more lower-level industrial jobs but sometimes better jobs with the prospect of advancement and higher pay. This accomplishment narrowed the large gaps between whites and blacks in occupational status and income. Roughly 10 percent of the population, blacks held just 3 percent of defense jobs in 1942, but more than 8 percent by 1945. As the number of black workers rose by 20 percent (by about one million) during the war, the number of black foremen, craftsmen, and operatives doubled. The number of African-American civilian employees of the federal government more than tripled, from 60,000 to 200,000, and increasingly they attained higher job classifications. In terms of black occupational status and income levels, World War II has been called "the turning point" for black Americans by one careful study, a time when African-American workers "for the first time took a giant step toward equality with whites."

But neither the relative nor the absolute gains should be exaggerated. The great increases in desirable jobs came in the industrial and occupational categories that expanded most rapidly during the war—in just those jobs where there was at once the largest need for workers, the smallest challenge to established white workers, and the greatest vulnerability to layoffs when the war was over. Very small gains came in professional, managerial, and white-collar jobs. African Americans remained hugely overrepresented among service workers and unskilled industrial and agricultural workers at the bottom of the occupational hierarchy. The combination of job and wage differentials left black median income about half that of whites. And the occupational gains for black men seem to have been largely the result of migration to the North and West, where there was more opportunity. While the overall ratio of nonwhite to white occupational status nationwide rose slightly, there was virtually no change region by region.

In a number of ways migration was central to the impact of the war on African Americans. The exodus of blacks from the rural South catalyzed by World War I but dampened by the Great Depression began again with renewed vigor in the middle of the war as jobs began to open up, and then continued powerfully into the postwar era. In all, an estimated 700,000 black civilians moved during the war, especially toward the same Northern and Western industrial areas as other migrants. Peaking from 1943 to 1945, black migration increased the African-American population of the ten largest war production centers by 49 percent, far greater than the total 19 percent population increase there. More than half of young black veterans lived in a different section of the country in 1950 than where they had been born. In 1940, 49 percent of blacks were urban; in 1950 the figure was 62 percent. The proportion of African Americans living in the South declined from 77 to 68 percent in the same period.

Migration brought troubles as well as opportunity. Crowded and dilapidated housing, deficient social services, hostile local officials and police, segregation by law in the South and by custom elsewhere, and white antipathy typically greeted inmigrant blacks. Wartime migration sometimes put almost impossible strains on available housing, transportation, and recreational facilities and brought suspicious racial and ethnic groups into contact. Particularly in the summer of 1943, as black migration and occupational advances grew noticeably, a number of race riots occurred, some in and around military training camps, some in urban areas.

The worst came in Detroit and New York. Racial tensions, especially over housing, had marked wartime Detroit from the beginning. In June 1943 a series of relatively minor incidents and then rumors of murder and rape by both blacks and whites produced a full-scale race riot of mutual aggression that left twenty-five blacks and nine whites dead and almost seven hundred people injured. In August blacks rioted in Harlem, aiming their anger at white institutions and property. The riot, which reflected long-simmering social, economic, and institutional resentments and was touched off by false rumors that a white policeman had killed a black GI, left six dead, all African Americans, and some three hundred injured.

Stemming from long-standing patterns of American race relations and from wartime change and tension, the riots also reflected the divergent outlooks of black and white Americans. Throughout the war, what was called black "morale"— in particular, the enthusiasm of African Americans for the war effort—was closely watched by black leaders and the government alike. Some African Americans seemed to take pleasure in Japanese military successes against whites and professed skepticism about the "white man's war." Responding much less favorably to anti-Japanese propaganda, blacks typically assigned a lower priority to the Pacific war than did whites. But there was little real identification with the Japanese; what sometimes seemed to be pro-Japanese sentiment really reflected resentment and frustration at circumstances in America. Black Americans overwhelmingly supported the war effort and wanted full participation in it and in the opportunities of American life.

But the loyalty and desire to serve that characterized black attitudes during the war years clearly involved different priorities and perceptions than those of white Americans. When polled in 1942, African Americans in New York and Memphis split almost evenly as to whether victory abroad over the Axis or victory at home over Jim Crow should have priority. Black protest became far more visible in wartime America— not only the Double V campaign and the March on Washington Movement but also picketing, boycotts, and other direct-action campaigns, especially by younger people organized by the new interracial Congress of Racial Equality (CORE). The National Association for the Advancement of Colored People (NAACP), the foremost civil rights organization, grew almost tenfold during the war, from some fifty thousand members to nearly half a million. Even in the oppressive and dangerous Mississippi Delta, observers noted that black leaders were "becoming more fearless and ready to state what they believe to be the basic rights of the group."

While African Americans grew more restive, polls early in the war showed that a substantial majority of whites thought that blacks were satisfied with things as they were, were finding sufficient opportunity, and should do more to help themselves. There were predictable regional differences, with Northerners more likely to perceive black dissatisfaction and to support change by way of better jobs and enhanced opportunity in the military. Southerners, clinging to old racial mores, bitterly opposed change and evidence of black assertiveness and autonomy. Regardless of region, most white Americans early in the war believed in segregation on the battlefront and the home front alike—in housing, restaurants, schools, and the armed forces. And if white Southerners were alarmed about wartime racial change, so too were many white Northerners, particularly working-class whites in the crowded war production centers.

Reflecting the explosive wartime amalgam of racial tensions, the race riots also changed things, at least in some ways. Many African-American leaders and organizations, worried that violence would harm black prospects, increasingly counseled and practiced greater moderation—though the ebbing of militance also reflected real gains in the military and in defense jobs. More important in the long run, the riots helped bring home to many whites the real dissatisfactions and thus the true circumstances of African Americans. In one 1942 poll three-fifths of whites thought blacks were satisfied with things as they were; the same polling agency in 1944 found that only one-fourth of whites thought blacks satisfied and more than half said they were not. Growing numbers of whites supported equal opportunities in jobs, education, and the armed forces, and Northern whites were more ready to

challenge the most visible and oppressive aspects of Jim Crow
in the South.

In the wake of the dreadful race riots of 1943 came numerous local and state interracial commissions. Organized to prevent violence and promote goodwill rather than to combat
discrimination, the commissions often concluded that the way
to prevent conflict was to address its root causes. Gunnar
Myrdal's influential 1944 book showing the contrast between
American principles and racial practices, *An American
Dilemma*, also helped change white perceptions and priorities.
In the North efforts began to implement fair-employment
policies. Nor did the war bring action only at the state and
local levels. In the military, in federal service, in the policies of
federal agencies, blacks received new attention. In 1944 the
Supreme Court, acting on a case brought by the NAACP, declared all-white Southern primaries unconstitutional. By the
end of the war, civil rights was part of the liberal policy
agenda.

In all, then, the war years were eventful and important ones
for black Americans. Looking back, Alexander J. Allen, an
African American who took part in wartime civil rights efforts with the Urban League, said that for him "the war period was a very compelling, very exhilarating era." And he
suggested more broadly that

> World War II was a watershed for blacks. Up to that point
> the doors to industrial and economic opportunity were
> largely closed. Under the pressures of the war, the pressures
> of governmental policy, the pressures of world opinion, the
> pressures of blacks themselves and their allies, all of this
> began to change. You get a new beginning in a sense....
> The war forced the federal government to take a stronger
> position with reference to discrimination, and things began
> to change as a result. There was also a tremendous attitudi-
> nal change that grew out of the war. There had been a new

experience for blacks, and many weren't willing to go back
to the way it was before.

War's end saw some threats to these advances, efforts to return to how things had been. Last hired, black workers were
often the first fired, and black veterans had more trouble than
whites in using the GI Bill. Black veterans and activists were
the victims of racial violence in the postwar South as whites
used both the law and lawlessness in an effort to reimpose old
racial norms. At a Baltimore war plant it was reported that
whites "universally" said that "when the war is over, we are
going to have to fight another one against the Negroes" to
keep the best jobs. In 1945 Congress halved the FEPC's budget and provided for its demise in 1946, and the Truman administration seemed at first a weak force for civil rights.
African Americans thus remained subject to the oppressive
Jim Crow regime in the South and to a variety of discriminatory patterns elsewhere.

Yet the momentum of the war years—in government and
the military, in employment, in the changing agenda of white
liberals, and above all in black activism and protest and the
day-to-day frustrations and rising expectations of ordinary
African Americans—persisted into the postwar years, laying
a crucial groundwork for the civil rights era to follow. For
blacks more clearly than for women, connections can be
drawn between wartime experience and postwar protest and
change. As one black GI put it, "After the close of hostilities,
we just kept on fighting. It's just that simple."

For women and African Americans, the questions of
World War II as a decisive turning point and as the Good War
are open to debate. Clearly the war brought new opportunities
to both groups and important new experiences and expectations. Men and women began to change their minds about

what women could do; many white Americans came to a new understanding about the conditions and frustrations of black Americans, and some began to support civil rights initiatives. But for women and African Americans, wartime developments also continued or reinforced prewar trends and patterns, and failed to dispel powerful traditional stereotypes and constraints. For both groups the wartime experience posed fundamental questions about inclusiveness, equal rights, and what it meant to be an American. The war raised such questions for other groups as well.

6

"Americans All"?

WARTIME AMERICA has seemed aptly characterized by the phrase "Americans All"—a diverse people united to defeat the Axis. Every squad and every ship's compartment, so it has seemed in memory and the movies, had someone named Kelly, and Goldstein, and Kowalski, and Jones, someone named Tonelli, and Larsen, and Sanchez, and Schmidt, perhaps even an Indian called "chief"—Americans all, from Brooklyn and Dixie and from all across the land, joined in common cause. The shared experiences and values of the war years have been credited with accelerating the acceptance, assimilation, and advance of the nation's minority groups.

Perhaps paradoxically, the celebrated unity of wartime America has been connected to efforts during the war to respect cultural pluralism and to protect differing views. But there were significant and sometimes glaring exceptions. The best known was the wartime relocation and incarceration of more than 100,000 Japanese Americans, some two-thirds of them native-born American citizens. African Americans were only slowly and partially made part of the war effort at home and abroad. And there was other evidence of division, exclusion, and conflict in wartime America, most of it deeply rooted, as well as efforts to force uniformity and muzzle dissent. How far, then, was World War II the Good War of healthy unity, pluralism, mutual respect, and protection of civil liberties? What difference did the war make in the lives of individuals and groups who, like women and African Americans, were in one way or another on the margins of American society?

"Enemy Alien" Groups

The experiences of ethnic groups from the Axis nations at war with America—Germany, Italy, and Japan—help to answer those questions. For Italian Americans the war was a trying but ultimately positive experience that helped bring them into the mainstream of American life; for German Americans the war years largely confirmed their prewar assimilation and acceptance; for Japanese Americans the war brought a traumatic denial of civil liberties. The far different experience of Japanese Americans has often been attributed to the single factor of race. But while race was the central theme, it was not the whole story, which must be told in the larger setting of the dynamics and patterns of American society.

At the outset of World War II the United States had changed from a generation earlier in ways that militated against a repetition of World War I's repressive campaigns for Americanism and Americanization. In 1940 unnaturalized immigrants—"aliens" in the technical term—were just 3 percent of the population, as against 7 percent in 1920. With the sharp reduction of immigration after the restrictive immigration legislation of 1924, most immigrants had been in the country for at least two decades. The nation's immigrants were thus far more acculturated than they had been during World War I, and their children and grandchildren were better assimilated into American society.

Beyond such simple but important demographic patterns were important ideological factors. For one thing, American policymakers and many of the American people recalled the excesses of the World War I home front, including the shameful treatment of German Americans, with a determination not to repeat such an episode. For another, developments in the social sciences during the interwar years had gone far toward eroding intellectual foundations for racism and ethnocentrism and had laid important groundwork for respecting minority groups and cultural pluralism. For yet another, World War II, at least after Pearl Harbor, was a war of unified common cause in a way that World War I had not been. And World War II was often understood not only as a war for democracy but also as a war against Nazi Germany and its master-race philosophy.

Even so, the United States, especially before Pearl Harbor, was marked by important ethnic divisions and tensions. The nation was not quite a melting pot, nor were immigrant institutions and organizations unimportant relics. While generally much less rigid than the color line, ethnic differences remained powerful, particularly for such groups as the Asian and Spanish-speaking minorities in the West who were at the juncture of race and ethnicity. For the so-called "new immigrants" from southern and eastern Europe—Italians, Poles, and East European Jews in particular—ethnic communities and organizations were central to group life and solidarity. For them, but also for such older and less segregated groups as the Germans, churches and schools, lodges and mutual aid societies, shops and festivals, foreign-language newspapers and radio stations, and group intramarriage all preserved ethnic consciousness and elements of the old ways.

Ethnicity also figured in the occupational and economic stratification of prewar America. Old-stock whites of northern and western European roots typically held the most powerful and lucrative positions in the national economy, with new immigrant Italians, Poles, and others largely clustered in insecure, low-paying, low-status blue-collar jobs. Professional occupations were disproportionately held by old-stock white Protestants and increasingly by Jews, while British immigrants, Irish, Germans, Jews, and Scandinavians tended to fill in the middle ranks of skilled blue-collar and lower-status white-collar workers. Germans and Scandinavians also predominated among Midwestern farmers, while Western agriculture employed Hispanic and Japanese farm workers. Social and economic differences and cultural bias found expression in such instruments of the popular culture as films and mass-circulation magazines, which typically featured attractive, successful old-stock "Americans" but portrayed minorities with such patronizing stereotypes as the "Italian gangster" or the "sly and shrewd Jew."

During the 1930s group conflict occasionally flared as old antagonisms were exacerbated by the depression and the coming of war. With the Nazi conquest of western Europe in the spring of 1940 and Italy's declaration of war against France in June, tensions mounted. Sure that spies and saboteurs had weakened western Europe, some Americans expressed alarm about the possibility of similar "fifth column" activities in the United States. Concern focused especially on German Americans and Italian Americans.

Such fears were essentially groundless. Despite lingering ties to the old country, German Americans and Italian Americans were with virtual unanimity loyal Americans. German Americans quickly moved away from any identification with Hitler and Nazi Germany. Better assimilated than the Italian Americans, German Americans also vividly remembered their traumatic World War I experience. As Hitler's intentions became clearer, such ideological and political support as he had won among German Americans—always small—largely vanished. Although typically opposed to anti-Axis policy, German Americans became increasingly critical of the

Nazis and more forceful in their declarations of loyalty to the United States.

For Italian Americans the attachment to the homeland was closer and more deeply felt than that of the Germans. The largest of the "new immigrant" groups, the roughly 5 million Italian Americans included some 1.6 million immigrants in 1940, more than one-third of them not yet American citizens. Relatively unacculturated and unassimilated, frequently living in "Little Italies" in metropolitan areas, near the bottom of the economic ladder, they were often objects of prejudice and disdain. In a national poll taken in 1939, half of those with opinions said that Italian Americans made the worst citizens of all the immigrants; no other group came close. For their part, Italian Americans had in the 1930s found a sense of ethnic pride and vicarious prestige by identifying with Mussolini's impressive "New Italy." Partly a way to compensate for their status and circumstances in America, the attachment to Italy was mostly sentimental and visceral rather than ideological and was understandably stronger among the immigrant generation. Identification with Mussolini did not necessarily mean a rejection of America and rarely involved fascist beliefs. Rather, it typically reflected the conflicting identities and mixed loyalties—Italian or American?—of many Italian Americans.

Mussolini's invasion of France in June 1940 greatly complicated life for Italian Americans and exacerbated their sense of insecurity and marginality. Although they affirmed their American loyalty and sometimes denounced Mussolini, Italian Americans rarely renounced Italy, and some justified Italy's role. Roosevelt's much-publicized anti-Axis speech at Charlottesville, Virginia, where he angrily charged Mussolini with having stabbed France in the back, profoundly disturbed Italian Americans. Not only did it seem to portend war against their homeland, but the president had evoked the derogatory image of the supposed Italian fondness for the stiletto.

The war in Europe also made ethnic voting more apparent and important in 1940. Concerned about their homelands and their folk abroad, American ethnic groups approached foreign policy and politics with particular interest and intensity in 1940, as their high voting rates indicated. On opposite sides of the political spectrum were Jews, who for the most part strongly favored an interventionist policy even at the risk of war and whose vote remained overwhelmingly Democratic, and the Germans and Italians, who generally opposed intervention and who voted in dramatically smaller proportions for Roosevelt and the Democrats than they had in 1936.

These political responses reinforced fears of old-country loyalties and of possible "fifth-column" espionage and sabotage among alien groups. In May 1940 FDR had authorized wiretaps on "persons suspected of subversive activities," and in telling Attorney General Robert H. Jackson to limit their use instructed him to restrict the wiretaps "insofar as possible to aliens." In June Congress passed the Smith Act, which among other things required that aliens register, be fingerprinted, and list their organizational affiliations. It also provided for the deportation of any aliens who had ever belonged to a Communist or fascist group. Suspicion of aliens and foreign-stock groups in the tense atmosphere of 1940–1941 also appeared in economic discrimination. Defense contractors especially went beyond official policy that barred aliens from certain jobs, and sometimes refused to hire anyone who seemed "foreign." In Hartford, Connecticut, one Justice Department investigator found, defense industries hired no blacks, no aliens, and "no persons of German and very few of Italian ancestry." The congressman from heavily Italian New

Haven reported a "wave of sentiment" against Italians, manifested in part by firing them "out of sheer spite and for malicious reasons."

Such practices worried the Roosevelt administration for two practical reasons. First, particularly by 1941 there was a growing need for war workers, and ethnic discrimination threatened to reduce the employment pool in crucial areas. Second, such discrimination seemed likely to erode the morale and perhaps even the loyalty of the ethnic groups involved. In fact, discrimination against ethnic groups typically concerned many government officials in 1941 more than did discrimination against African Americans and was an important part of the reason for Executive Order 8802 and the establishment of the Fair Employment Practices Committee in June 1941. After Pearl Harbor, FDR publicly labeled discrimination against aliens and immigrants "stupid" and "unjust," and noted that discriminatory employers "are engendering the very distrust and disunity on which our enemies are counting to defeat us." The administration continued to press hard, through the FEPC and other agencies, to help ethnic groups counter discrimination and find appropriate jobs.

But that general effort did not resolve the question of what to do about unnaturalized immigrants from the Axis nations. At first there was no fundamental policy distinction made between Italian, German, and Japanese aliens. After Pearl Harbor all were designated "enemy aliens," and all were subject to restrictions on possessions (including short-wave radios and cameras) and on personal movement (especially near vital or seemingly vulnerable defense areas). Enemy aliens were liable for apprehension, restraint, detention, and deportation and had to carry special identification. In the winter of 1941–1942 some officials in Washington contemplated the wholesale relocation and even detention of Italian and German as well as Japanese aliens throughout the nation.

From the first, however, Japanese Americans were in fact treated differently. Japanese aliens were more likely to be on government watch lists and to be interned. Ultimately more than 100,000 Japanese Americans, most of them native-born American citizens, were removed from the West Coast and placed in relocation camps. By contrast, German and Italian aliens did not experience mass relocation, detention, or internment, and the Italians were even removed from the enemy alien category within a year of Pearl Harbor. Action against German-American and Italian-American citizens received no serious consideration.

Developments on the West Coast clarify the larger national story. At first General John L. DeWitt, head of the Western Defense Command, reflecting the views of many local officials and citizens as well as the fears of the military, wanted to relocate all enemy aliens. Early in 1942 several thousand Italians and Germans were ordered to leave coastal security zones and thus their homes and jobs until permitted to return in the summer. But it was clear that mass removal of Italians and Germans would pose major logistical problems and would jeopardize California's economy and the morale of the larger Italian-American and German-American communities. The prospects of removing and detaining all of America's 599,000 Italian and 264,000 German aliens raised such concerns to enormous levels nationwide.

By the spring of 1942 the idea of mass relocations of Italian and German aliens had been abandoned. Democratic principle and a concern about civil liberties played a role in this outcome, as did continuing feelings of guilt about the treatment of the Germans during World War I. So too did the absence of any significant disloyalty and of any real military or security threat or fifth-column action. But practical reasons were important, especially the large numbers of German and Italian aliens involved and the economic and morale difficulties that mass removals would entail. And both German Americans and Italian Americans constituted large voting blocs with powers of protection and retribution.

Both groups, moreover, seemed to most Americans not to pose threats to national unity or the war effort. Although polls in 1941 and 1942 revealed some suspicion and fear of German aliens, the larger German-American population was by World War II not only acculturated but largely assimilated and accepted. (Symptomatic of the status of German Americans was the absence of concern about the leading role in the European theater played by General Dwight D. Eisenhower, with his obviously German name.) Italian Americans were less in the mainstream of American life than the Germans, but they were far more acculturated, assimilated, and accepted than the Japanese and were not so much feared as disdained. Like the Germans, they were whites of European origin.

The treatment and status of German Americans during the war largely corroborated their assimilation over the previous several decades and the acceptance and goodwill they had won. Some tension appeared among German Americans; some were suspect and found their children taunted; and many German-American families deliberately avoided speaking German or teaching it to their sons and daughters. Yet the war was not so much a turning point for them as it was a confirmation of their status as Americans.

For Italian Americans the World War II experience was more fundamentally important. Even before Pearl Harbor almost half of Italian aliens had applied for citizenship. After Pearl Harbor, Italian Americans, aliens and citizens alike, demonstrated that Italian was only the modifier, American the basic noun—that they were by identity and loyalty Americans. They contributed vitally to the military and to defense production. Anti-Italian suspicion and prejudice did not entirely abate, and Italian-American children often shared the anxieties of their elders and were subject to insults. But as Italian Americans declared and demonstrated their Americanism, they were increasingly accepted by the larger society. Basic demographic and social dynamics were leading in that direction already, especially as Italian Americans became increasingly a second- and even third-generation group. Economic advance, political power, social acceptance—all those were already on the way. Still, World War II hastened the process.

On Columbus Day 1942 FDR removed Italians from the enemy alien category. He hoped the action might help American propaganda in Italy and thus the war effort; and remembering the sharp falloff in the Democratic vote among Italians in 1940, and concerned about the outcome of the 1942 congressional elections, Roosevelt took his action on the great Italian-American holiday—conveniently just a few weeks before the elections. Still, whatever its several purposes, FDR's action was an apt recognition of Italian-American loyalty and contributions and a symbol of their acceptance.

For Japanese Americans the wartime experience was far different. Of the 127,000 Japanese Americans in the continental United States, some 80,000 were Nisei, native-born American citizens; another 47,000 were Issei, unnaturalized Japanese immigrants who were prohibited by U.S. law from becoming citizens and whose alien status was thus no necessary indication of their loyalty or identity. But even as the idea of the mass relocation of Italian and German aliens was being dropped, it was decided to remove and detain in relocation camps the entire Japanese-American population—men, women, and children, citizens and aliens alike—of California, Washington, Oregon, and part of Arizona.

Race was the foremost factor, but a number of other reasons help to explain why Japanese Americans were treated so much differently from the Germans and Italians. There were relatively few of them, so their removal and incarceration did not raise massive logistical problems. They had very little real or potential political power, either in Washington or in the West. Concentrated in agriculture, domestic service, and ethnic businesses, they did not play a vital role in defense industries or in the regional or national economies. Their relative isolation in tight, separate communities helped perpetuate ignorance, prejudice, and unrealistic fears.

Such circumstances also help explain the different treatment accorded Japanese Americans in Hawaii, where military and security reasons given for relocation were surely more compelling. Although some individuals considered dangerous were detained and hundreds—most of them American citizens—were sent to the mainland, it was decided early in 1942 not to attempt mass relocation or detention of the Japanese on Hawaii. The 150,000 people of Japanese ancestry on the islands made up more than one-third of the population and thus posed considerable logistical problems of relocation or internment. They were vital to Hawaii's economy. Martial law in the islands probably reduced anxieties, and in any case Hawaii was a territory, not a state, and thus its anti-Japanese residents did not have the sort of power in national politics that their counterparts on the West Coast could exercise. Finally, the Japanese on Hawaii were part of a multiracial society and not the objects of such intense fears or prejudice as the mainland Japanese.

While race was not the only factor leading to the mass removals and incarceration of West Coast Japanese Americans, it was central to what happened. They had long been the victims not just of ignorance, prejudice, and discrimination in hiring and housing but also of state and local laws barring their intermarriage with whites, excluding them from swimming pools and dance halls, and denying them the right to vote and own land. The attack on Pearl Harbor energized those on the West Coast long concerned about the "yellow peril" as well as economic competitors in agriculture and small business.

Understandable but exaggerated and often irrational military fears whipped up animosity against the Japanese on the West Coast. (National polls in the spring and summer of 1942 in fact showed that German aliens were thought to be more dangerous than Japanese aliens.) Ironically, the very absence of real evidence of espionage or sabotage raised fears on the coast—the Japanese, it was thought, were almost diabolically clever in masking their intentions and actions and their devotion to the emperor. Speaking not only for the army but for local officials and much of the public, General DeWitt said, "A Jap's a Jap.... It makes no difference whether he is an American citizen or not.... I don't want any of them.... There is no way to determine their loyalty." In any case, he said, "racial affinities are not severed by migration. The Japanese race is an enemy race." A newspaper columnist wrote, "Herd 'em up, pack 'em off... let 'em be pinched, hurt, hungry and dead up against it ... I hate the Japanese."

Washington resisted mass relocation at first, but wildly exaggerated military fears, pressure from Western officials and citizens, the preferences of Secretary of War Stimson and army Provost Marshal General Allen W. Gullion (though not of army Chief of Staff Marshall), and the absence of the factors protecting the Germans and Italians ultimately led FDR to acquiesce in the removals. On February 19, 1942, the president issued Executive Order 9066, authorizing the War Department to designate "military areas" from which anyone might be excluded. Secretary of War Stimson implemented the order only on the West Coast and only against Japanese Americans. The mass evacuation began in March.

By September more than 100,000 Japanese Americans had been uprooted from homes and jobs, effectively stripped of most of their property along with their rights, and incarcerated in camps run by the War Relocation Authority (WRA) headed by Milton S. Eisenhower, the general's brother. Located in remote areas and surrounded by barbed wire, the camps had tar-papered wooden barracks, primitive conditions, and communal bathing, toilet, and eating facilities offering little privacy or dignity. Parents and older people saw their status and authority vanish, and dissension, distrust, and depression were commonplace. Several thousand renounced their American citizenship, and some 18,000 disgruntled and allegedly "disloyal" Japanese Americans were moved to Tule Lake in California. Riots occurred in a number of the camps, most notably at Manzanar in 1942.

At first seen as temporary relocation centers by the WRA, the camps became more permanent wartime residences for most of the interned Japanese Americans. By 1943 individuals whose loyalty was not in question could leave upon evidence of a job and community acceptance awaiting them. By the end of 1944 some 35,000 people had left the camps. Then, in early 1945, with the end of the war in sight, the government permitted everyone deemed loyal to depart. Many were at first reluctant, even fearful, to do so, but ultimately they were compelled to leave. Initially the evacuees were given minimal assistance, then they were left on their own.

The entire episode, as Secretary Stimson had observed at the outset, made "a tremendous hole in our constitutional system." Japanese Americans had posed no real military or security threat, but citizens and aliens alike had been stripped of their rights and property because of public and political pressure, because of fear, because it was practicable, and because of race. Some critics spoke out, especially toward the end of the war, but both liberals and conservatives acquiesced in the relocations on the grounds of military necessity, and the Supreme Court allowed the mass evacuation and incarceration.

This shattering experience for Japanese Americans arguably sped their entry into the mainstream of American society. After the war, societal guilt evidently helped reduce the obstacles and discrimination that Japanese Americans encountered—as did, no doubt, the splendid record of the 33,000 Japanese Americans who served in the armed forces. The Japanese-American 442nd Regimental Combat Team, in fact, was the army's most decorated unit. Partly because of the removals, Japanese Americans after the war pursued new opportunities and occupations in different, less enclosed and less isolated, communities. But the price of accelerating the acculturation and acceptance of Japanese Americans was individual trauma, group persecution, lingering resentment and psychic scars, several hundred million dollars in income and property losses, and gross violations of the constitutional rights of American citizens. In 1988 President Ronald Reagan signed congressional legislation that apologized for the incarceration and authorized payment of $20,000 to each surviving Japanese American who had been in the camps.

OTHER MINORITY GROUPS

For most minority groups the war years brought a greater inclusion into the social and economic mainstreams of American life. Prewar developments in anthropology and other social sciences had already undermined old notions of inherent ethnic hierarchies and had enhanced a sympathetic understanding of ethnicity and minority groups. During the war, the idea of cultural pluralism increasingly became part of the fabric of American life and American identity. The wartime "I Am an American Day" celebrations and related observances, though sharing some of the pressures for Americanization and denial of ethnic identity of World War I, typically were far more affirmative and inclusive events. Nearly two

million aliens, almost half the 1940 total, were naturalized
during the war; and while the motive was partly to avoid the
difficulties of "alien" status, the numbers also reflected accelerated patterns of American identity, acculturation, and acceptance. On the other hand, ethnic Americans did not plunge
headlong into the melting pot: metaphors of "orchestras" and
"salads" were common, metaphors reflecting a sense that differing parts made a stronger whole, that unity involved respect for diversity.

For Polish Americans, one of the largest of the "new immigrant" groups, the war years almost unobtrusively sped the
advances and assimilation that generational succession was
already producing. After the 1939 Nazi invasion of Poland,
Polish Americans avidly supported the war and became an essential and fully accepted part of the war effort. Many squads
and ships' compartments did in fact have someone called
"Ski," as did factory floors in the major war industries. The
insistent Polish-American concern about Soviet intentions
and the future of Poland expressed toward the end of the war
raised no questions about Polish-American loyalty or identity,
for anxiety about the Soviet Union also became part of the
American consensus.

Other groups had more complicated and sometimes more
troubled wartime experiences. For Mexican Americans, by far
the most numerous of the nation's more than 1.5 million
Spanish-speaking people, the war years brought significant
change, enough that they have been called a "watershed" in
Mexican-American history. As with so many Americans, the
important wartime changes for Mexican Americans largely
involved jobs and residence. An estimated 350,000 Mexican
Americans served in the armed forces while others moved toward cities and defense jobs, especially in Western aircraft and
shipbuilding industries. Population movement away from enclosed rural and urban *barrios* and the new experiences, skills,

and training received in war plants and the armed forces
brought modernizing change to what had been largely an unskilled agricultural people on the margins of the regional and
national economies.

But the change was accompanied by tension and conflict,
especially in Western cities. Despite the contributions of Mexican Americans and their changing status during the war, they
remained at the intersection of ethnicity, race, and class, were
still subject to prejudice and discrimination, and lagged significantly behind in education, income, and occupational status.
Some younger people, alienated both from Anglo society and
from their parents' generation, joined the *pachuco* gangs of
Los Angeles and other cities. Like many other young Mexican
Americans, and African Americans too, the *pachucos* wore
"zoot suits"—a full coat reaching to mid-thigh, trousers flared
at the knee but tight at the ankles, thick-soled shoes, a felt
"pancake" hat, and a long key chain. In Los Angeles wartime
tensions, police harassment, and occasional *pachuco* attacks
on servicemen—typically over competition for Mexican-
American women—led to a series of clashes and incidents. In
the Los Angeles "zoot suit riot" of June 1943 sailors, claiming
revenge for assaults on them, attacked and beat Mexican
Americans while military and civilian police stood by. Fanned
by anti-Hispanic sentiments and an inflammatory press, similar incidents occurred in other cities.

California's governor appointed an investigating committee
which blamed the riots on wartime tensions, racial prejudice,
police unfairness, and an irresponsible press. In the aftermath
came a new appreciation of the difficulties faced by Mexican
Americans, and, partly out of a concern for relations with
Mexico, public and private efforts began throughout the region to reduce prejudice and enhance the economic and social
status of Mexican Americans. In addition to geographic and
economic change, then, the war years both focused attention

on the situation of Mexican Americans and heightened ethnic consciousness. Like black veterans, returning Mexican-American veterans often refused to acquiesce in old patterns of discrimination. The GI generation provided much of the postwar leadership for civil rights and economic and political progress for Mexican Americans in the West and Southwest.

For American Indians the war also brought—sometimes with significant differences from tribe to tribe—geographic and economic change, important participation in the war effort, new experiences and aspirations, and aggressive new leaders. And as with other groups, the war at once underwrote assimilation and ethnic assertiveness, a paradox consistent with the wartime blend of national unity and cultural pluralism. In 1940 most of the nation's 345,000 Native Americans lived depressed and dependent on reservations in the West, and though granted citizenship in 1924 (partly because of their record of volunteering for World War I), they still were denied the right to vote in several states.

Native Americans responded enthusiastically to the war effort. Military service took some 25,000 from tribal enclaves, gave them significant new experiences, led them to a heightened appreciation for training and education, and helped produce a generation of new leaders. Although Indians were almost inevitably called "chief" by their comrades, the term was more one of respect than insult; and the most common stereotype they encountered in the armed forces was an expectation that they would be especially brave and effective warriors. Navajo "code talkers" performed with extraordinary valor and effectiveness with the marines on the front lines of the bloody Pacific amphibious assaults. Important change came on the home front as well, as labor needs drew Indians to the cities and defense jobs. An estimated 40,000 thus contributed to the war effort at home, and like those in the military came away with new skills, experiences, and aspirations, a new sense of what the future might hold.

One major result of all this was to accelerate the ongoing process of detribalization and assimilation, though in complicated ways. Sometimes old tensions flared between reservation traditionalists and the younger generation's growing emphasis on training, education, and modernization. But across generations the war years also saw the revitalization of certain traditional ceremonials, especially those connected with combat, and more veterans and war workers than expected returned to reservations after the war. If the younger generation was more assimilationist, it was also often more assertive and sometimes militant with respect to Indian rights. Formed in 1944, the National Congress of American Indians played an important role in forwarding Indian rights in the postwar era.

Wartime experiences and expectations also contributed to ending the "Indian New Deal" of the 1930s and implementing the postwar "termination" policy by which the federal government relinquished its responsibility for Native Americans and moved toward terminating the reservation system. Underestimating the persisting importance of traditional ways and of tribal and reservation life for many, that policy contributed to the alienation and personal difficulties that continued to haunt Indians in the postwar era. Whether on the reservations or off, Indians encountered more social and economic problems than had seemed likely in the first optimistic flush of the wartime experience. World War II may have been the most important event in twentieth-century Indian history, as Alison R. Bernstein's thorough study suggests, but the impact of the war was often ambiguous and consistent with previous patterns.

For American Jews the war brought still another set of issues but, as with other minority groups, hastened assimilation even as it produced greater self-consciousness and self-

assertiveness. The war against the Nazis and the enormity of
the Holocaust went far toward discrediting anti-Semitism in
the United States and making Jews more aggressive in their
own defense and in defense of Jews abroad and in what became the state of Israel. Jews played important roles in the
American war effort, not least with the contribution of
refugee Jewish scientists to the atomic bomb project, and in
the process became more fully accepted by American society.
Already a group with significant political and economic assets,
American Jews by the end of the war also had additional
moral and ideological claims on full participation and fair
treatment. World War II sped the end of many of the discriminatory quotas and exclusions that had kept Jews from full
participation in the nation's economic and educational institutions.

Yet all this was not without the disturbing paradox of domestic anti-Semitism in the struggle against Hitler. Stereotypes persisted of the sly, selfish, and clannish Jew, and in
World War II as at other times of tension, Jews sometimes became scapegoats. Anti-Semitic diatribes and behavior were orchestrated before the war by the Nazi German-American
Bund and both before and during the war by Father Charles
Coughlin and his anti-Semitic followers; but anti-Semitism
extended well beyond those groups. Along with Italians, Jews
had encountered substantial prejudice and discrimination in
the 1930s, and the FEPC found job discrimination continuing against Jews during the war. Wartime opinion surveys
showed an increase in anti-Semitic feelings, including the
sense that Jews were profiting from the war and, though more
than a half-million served in the armed forces, were especially
successful in evading military service and combat. In Boston
and elsewhere on the East Coast, Jewish stores and syna-
gogues were vandalized, sometimes defaced with swastikas.

Ugly as such attitudes and behavior were, they tended to be

sporadic and to decline as the war proceeded. The greater harm of American anti-Semitism came not to American Jews but rather to European Jews who might have found refuge in the United States or protection from the American military. Despite growing evidence by the late 1930s of the Nazi persecution of Jews, anti-Semitism helped prevent easing U.S. immigration policy to admit Jewish refugees, and key State Department officials worked to restrict their entry. Perhaps 150,000 were admitted by 1942, a tragically small number. Acquiescing to politics, public opinion, and divided counsel on the issue, and during the war preoccupied with victory, Roosevelt also did much less than he might have done to rescue or assist Jews in Hitler's Europe. Indifference and anti-Semitic prejudice in the State Department, and the department's concern not to upset Arab nations by supporting a Jewish exodus to Palestine, contributed to American passivity. So did, even among Jewish leaders, an inability wholly to credit the mounting evidence of Nazi genocide and to agree upon policy. As a result, a potential haven for Jews was closed off, and the bombing of rail lines and concentration camps, which might at least have disrupted the mass exterminations that ultimately killed six million Jews, was never accomplished.

DISSENT AND DEVIANCE

The attack on Pearl Harbor produced an immediate closing of the ranks for wartime Americans and a shared understanding that the Allies were fighting a just war against totalitarian evil. The lack of fundamental protest or ideological division contributed not only to a unified war effort but also to one that generally honored democratic principles and civil liberties. Yet the story was not without its illuminating and sometimes surprising twists and exceptions.

At first, in the "fifth-column" fears of 1940 and 1941, it ap-

peared that some of the repressive reactions of World War I
might be repeated. The 1940 Smith Act not only imposed restrictions on aliens but made it illegal to conspire to teach or
advocate the violent overthrow of the government. That same
year Fritz Kuhn, leader of the German-American Bund, and
Earl Browder, head of the American Communist party, were
jailed for relatively minor infractions. Yet from the beginning
Roosevelt and the Justice Department were far more careful
about civil liberties than the Wilson administration had
been—partly because of painful memories of the World War
I home front. The administration generally sought to dimin-
ish public fears and incipient hysteria and to head off repressive legislation, even as it moved decisively, and reassuringly,
against sabotage and espionage.

The absence of dissent or protest from the left and the
wartime alliance with the Soviet Union went far toward protecting civil liberties in wartime America. American Communists supported the war effort after the German attack on the
USSR in June 1941, and the government and the media portrayed the Soviets as staunch and valued partners. *Life* magazine described the Russians as "one hell of a people" who
"look like Americans, dress like Americans and think like
Americans." In 1942 FDR pardoned Earl Browder, who remained throughout the war an insistent proponent of national
unity. Such overt anticommunism as existed was largely political, as in the red-baiting tactics of the 1944 Republican campaign.

To the degree that worrisome dissent might impair the war
effort, it came largely from the right. There the administration and its liberal supporters were not always solicitous of
freedom of expression. The White House worked behind the
scenes, for example, to have the Catholic hierarchy muzzle
Father Charles Coughlin, whose anti-Semitic writings and
speeches seemed a source of dangerous disruption and dis-

unity. In 1942 the Justice Department indicted more than two dozen "native fascists" for violating the 1917 Espionage Act by criticizing the government and thus conspiring to provoke insubordination in the armed forces. It was a weak case at best, mercifully ending in 1944 when the judge died and the administration moved for dismissal.

Black protest and its impact on the war effort also worried the White House. Roosevelt asked the Justice Department to talk with black newspaper editors "to see what could be done about preventing their subversive language"—such as the Double V campaign that condemned racism at home. No formal legal sanctions were applied, but the black press became less outspoken. Black protest and black nationalist groups were monitored by the Justice Department and were subject to charges of sedition or draft evasion, especially because some nationalist-separatist groups urged noncooperation with the "white man's war."

Another potential encroachment on civil liberties involved loyalty tests for federal workers. The 1939 Hatch Act had denied federal employment to anyone belonging to an organization that advocated the overthrow of the government, and during the war the Civil Service Commission's loyalty board greatly increased its operations and began routinely to inquire into the political beliefs of job applicants. In 1943 FDR reacted to charges of subversives in the government by creating the Interdepartmental Committee on Employee Investigations. Although it established a number of procedural safeguards, the committee used circumstantial as well as direct evidence of disloyalty and membership in "fellow-traveling" organizations as sufficient for an FBI investigation. Still, civil liberties were generally respected and protected on the World War II home front, certainly as compared with World War I or the other combatants in World War II.

So also were the rights of religiously motivated conscientious objectors. The Selective Service Act of 1940 excused from combat anyone who "by reason of religious training and belief is conscientiously opposed to participation in war in any form," and provided for either noncombatant military status or "work of national importance under civilian direction." Many members of the peace churches—Quakers, Brethren, and Mennonites—did not apply for exemption from military service, and most of the rest served as noncombatants, usually in the medical corps. Those who objected to any form of military service were put in public service camps where they worked without pay, especially in conservation and public health. Some of them, disliking the military supervision of the camps and feeling that in a total war even nonmilitary service contributed to the war effort and thus eroded their principles and moral witness, protested, but to no avail.

Those whose objection to military service did not emanate from accepted religious reasons met much less favorable government response. Moral or ethical opposition to war did not qualify, and men who refused to register for the draft or who objected on political grounds were sent to jail. In all, some 5,500 men were imprisoned, most of them Jehovah's Witnesses, who did not qualify as conscientious objectors because they did not oppose force in all circumstances. Some members of black nationalist groups who opposed service for racial reasons were convicted of draft evasion. The Supreme Court supported government policy—though the Court, in a case involving Jehovah's Witnesses, also barred states from enforcing a compulsory flag salute.

Homosexuals were another group for whom issues surrounding military service illuminated wartime American unity and conformity. In this case, of course, the question was one of behavior defined as deviant rather than ideological dissent or religious principle. Breaking with prewar practice, the United States alone among the belligerent nations screened for homosexuality during the military induction procedure. Before the war homosexual acts were grounds for courts-martial, but during the war psychiatrists held that homosexuality constituted a personality type unfit for military service. In addition to a few thousand men disqualified for entry into the armed forces, several thousand servicemen were treated as homosexual psychiatric cases and given the "blue" discharge that went to other "undesirables" such as drug addicts and thieves. After the war, proscriptions against gays in the military became routinized, they were sometimes denied GI Bill benefits, and homosexuality became an important source of investigation for security risks.

Yet there was more to the wartime experience than that. The screening upon entry into the armed forces was notoriously inexact and lax, and action against gays and lesbians in the military was taken only occasionally—partly because it threatened to reduce available personnel for the armed forces. Of some eighteen million people screened for military service, less than an infinitesimal three-hundredths of 1 percent were rejected for homosexuality, and a comparably tiny fraction of those in the service were removed. Thus many homosexuals served effectively in the armed forces during World War II.

The war years also provided homosexuals a chance for personal self-discovery and group solidarity. In the flux and mobility of wartime America, away from old familial and community constraints, amidst the generally freer sexual behavior of the war years, and perhaps especially in the sex-segregated armed forces, gay men and lesbians discovered themselves and others like them. They found opportunities to pursue their sexual orientations, and though sometimes targets of persecution in the military, they found strength and solace in the other homosexual GIs they met. For innumerable homosexuals, then, on the home front as well as the battle-front, the war years were a time of developments that would help establish a larger and more assertive gay subculture in the postwar years. For homosexuals too, the war years have thus been seen as a turning point, with significant departures in national policy and in gay individual and group experience.

The phrase "Americans All" was more than just a slogan during World War II. To a substantial degree, wartime Americans united in common cause across the various fault lines of American society. For women and African Americans, for most ethnic groups, for homosexuals as well, the war also brought new circumstances that laid foundations for further change and assertiveness in the postwar era. And wartime America allowed leeway for most conscientious objectors and experienced nothing like the repressive campaigns for loyalty and correct behavior that had marked the World War I home front. But the story was by no means entirely positive; the war years also saw divisions and polarities that produced tension, sometimes conflict, and for some a denial of constitutional rights.

Long-range perspectives suggest that much of the change and most of the patterns of the war years were a consequence of important continuities from the past. Certainly racial and ethnic prejudice and fears of disloyalty, dissent, and deviance had roots in the past; but so too did the emphasis on democracy and diversity, and the growing acculturation and acceptance of white ethnic groups was in part a function of time and demography.

7

"Politics as Usual"

DURING THE 1942 elections Republicans and Democrats accused each other of "politics as usual." In the midst of a global war in which the tide had not yet clearly turned for the Allies, "politics as usual" was a pejorative term, signifying that narrow partisanship afflicted politics and policymaking when the nation needed patriotic unity of purpose. But while there was surely much partisan and personal self-seeking in the politics of wartime America, the phrase "politics as usual" described the war years in two other ways as well.

For one thing, American democratic processes continued throughout the war. In contrast even to England, which formed a wartime coalition government and called off regular elections for the duration, the normal political rhythms prescribed by the American constitution proceeded unabated. Whatever the sharp and often shrill partisanship, wartime politics were both symbol and reality of American democracy—politics as usual despite national emergency. Not only the processes but also the substance of national politics changed relatively little. World War II transformed the context of American politics, but the basic lineaments of prewar voting patterns, domestic policy, and even party issues and images persisted powerfully through the war years. Rather than wrenching politics from their prewar channels, the war tended to deepen the new political contours of the 1930s and make them more permanent features of American life.

THE ELECTION OF 1940

American politics in 1940 contrasted sharply with those of just a decade earlier. The New Deal regulatory-welfare state had greatly increased the size and power of the federal government, and politics pivoted more than before on ideology, with Democrats generally the liberal party of big, reformist central government, Republicans the party of conservatism, limited government, and localism. The impact of the Great Depression, the activism and help of the New Deal, and the leadership and personality of Franklin D. Roosevelt had by the mid-1930s made the Democrats—a seemingly hopeless minority in the 1920s—the nation's majority party. In 1936 Roosevelt won a reelection victory of unprecedented magnitude by carrying 60.8 percent of the popular vote and all but two states, and helping Democrats win top-heavy majorities in both houses of Congress.

The "Roosevelt coalition" of voters that provided the new Democratic majority reflected important divides in prewar America. As they had for decades, Democrats found great support among white Southerners and among Catholic immigrant groups while Republicans continued to have particular strength among old-stock white Protestants throughout the North. The 1930s brought Democrats new majority support from Jews and African Americans, but perhaps of even greater significance was the increased importance of ideology and class in national politics. Appreciative of New Deal assistance and economic security, working-class and lower-income voters sided overwhelmingly with the Democrats while upper-income voters, preferring less government to more, voted heavily Republican. White-collar and middle-income voters and farmers divided more evenly but tended in the mid-1930s to support Roosevelt and the New Deal. In 1936 FDR won nearly four-fifths of the lower-income vote, three-fifths of the middle, and two-fifths of the upper.

Despite the sweeping Democratic victory of 1936, however, Republicans retained considerable potential power, as did traditional conservative and antistatist opposition to big government. Much of the support for the New Deal had involved approval of specific programs with tangible benefits rather than an ideological conversion to taxing, spending, planning, and the welfare state. Then a series of events—the 1937 "court-packing" proposal (by which Roosevelt sought to gain a friendly majority on the Supreme Court by adding justices), labor unrest, and the sharp 1937–1938 recession in particular—fueled conservative resistance to new New Deal measures among Republicans and conservative Democrats alike and sparked sharp Republican gains in the 1938 elections. Although Democrats remained the majority party in Congress, an emerging coalition of Republicans and conservative, mostly Southern, Democrats foiled efforts to expand the New Deal and sometimes managed to trim existing programs in the late 1930s.

The New Deal party system that emerged in the 1930s received its first major challenge during the war years. As prosperity replaced depression, as new ethnic concerns surfaced, as foreign policy gained new importance, the political context that had produced the New Deal and the new Democratic majority changed dramatically. Repercussions in the United States of the Nazi conquest of western Europe and the Battle of Britain made the 1940 presidential election really the first wartime election. Galvanizing the national defense program and with it American production, employment, and income, events in Europe intensified the ongoing debate between interventionists and isolationists and began clearly to swing the tide toward those who wanted, short of war, to help Great Britain against the Axis.

Perhaps the war's most significant impact on the election was in helping determine the presidential nominees. At the beginning of the year Roosevelt seemed uncertain of his intentions, and polls indicated that a majority of voters would oppose an unprecedented third term. In the GOP, Manhattan's aggressive young district attorney Thomas E. Dewey and Ohio's conservative Senator Robert A. Taft were the apparent front-runners. Then came the Nazi spring *blitzkrieg*. The global situation evidently convinced Roosevelt—or, some would say, afforded him a pretext—to seek reelection in order to implement a pro-Allied foreign policy. It also turned public opinion around on a third term. By May nearly three-fifths of those polled said they would support FDR for another four years in the White House. Roosevelt won easy renomination.

Global affairs also helped crystallize the GOP's decision. With Dewey seeming too young and Taft too inflexibly isolationist, sentiment mounted for a man who at first seemed to have no real chance: Wendell L. Willkie. A man of great talent and energy from small-town Indiana, Willkie had headed a major utilities company and won attention in the late 1930s as an engaging champion of private enterprise and initiative against New Deal regulation and spending. Promoted by a remarkable media campaign orchestrated by the Luce publications, the magnetic Willkie shot from dark horse to serious contender by the time of the GOP convention and won nomination on the sixth ballot.

Crucial to the presidential nominations, the war also figured in the campaign. Willkie initially supported Roosevelt's increasingly pro-Allied foreign policy, including the new conscription bill and aid to Great Britain. But as the campaign wore on and his chances faded, Willkie backed off and charged repeatedly that reelecting Roosevelt would inevitably and quickly mean war for the United States. Fearful that Willkie's charges of war might stampede nervous and noninterventionist voters to the GOP camp, including Germans, Italians, and Anglophobic Irish opposed to pro-Allied policy, Roosevelt toward the end issued his famous pledge in Boston: "I have said this before, but I shall say it again and again and again: Your boys are not going to be sent into any foreign wars."

Yet for all that the question of war and foreign policy hung over American life in 1940 and powerfully affected politics for the first time in a generation, domestic issues rather than those of war and defense predominated in the campaign. In the media perhaps three-fourths of the campaign coverage dealt with domestic issues, and Roosevelt and his eight-year domestic record provided the main focus of the campaign. From the beginning Willkie attacked the president for economic defeatism, excessive centralization, persisting economic problems, and inadequate defense preparations—all issues that involved Willkie's central theme of the power of unfettered private enterprise. "Only the strong can be free," said Willkie throughout the campaign, and "only the productive can be strong." Although he supported such "minimum guarantees" of the New Deal as collective bargaining, Social Security, and the minimum wage, Willkie attacked Roosevelt for underestimating the potential of the American economy and aggrandizing the power of government. Their chief difference, he said, was that "the New Deal candidate does not believe that there are any more jobs, whereas I know there are." Willkie pledged to unleash the dynamic private-enterprise economy. He claimed the result would be prosperity with "new employment—more jobs—more work—more growth—more expansion" and "a new America with a higher standard of life than we have dreamed of before."

Roosevelt offered a different approach to a similar future.

Pointing to gains in production, jobs, profits, income, and living standards under his administration—gains especially sharp in 1940 because of the impact of defense spending—FDR declared that his objective in the next four years was "to make work for every young man and woman in America a living fact." But his emphasis on the role of government to ensure security, employment, and "social and economic justice" for all Americans differed from Willkie's insistence on an expanding private-enterprise economy. FDR warned of those who offer "extravagant promises of fabulous wealth," who "try to delude us with a mirage on the far horizon—a mirage of an island of dreams, with palaces and palms and plums."

By the next presidential election, the postwar program of FDR and the liberal Democrats would come far closer to Willkie's vision of the near-limitless possibilities of jobs and higher living standards in a dynamic American economy than most would have guessed during the 1940 campaign. But in November 1940 the electorate cast up a judgment that was shaped more by memories of the recent past and a practical concern about the present than by grand visions of the future, and more by the domestic experience of the preceding decade than by the drama abroad. Nor were many voters deflected by Republican charges that Roosevelt's try for an unprecedented third term portended dictatorship in America.

Roosevelt won his third term with 54.8 percent of the vote and thirty-eight of the forty-eight states, and Democrats easily retained control of Congress. Significantly the election returns closely conformed to 1936 patterns. FDR's greatest strength again came from the South, from urban areas, and from lower-income, ethnic, and black voters. The 1940 election was thus of great importance in solidifying the political patterns and the new majority Roosevelt coalition of the 1930s.

The European war did have its effect on voting in 1940.

One of every four 1936 Roosevelt supporters who voted again in 1940 voted for Willkie, and Democratic defections were particularly striking among isolationists and among such groups as the German Americans and Italian Americans who opposed FDR's anti-Axis policy. The war also helped shore up Roosevelt's support. Public concern about the war and national security gave the president a clear edge in November as the man better able to protect the nation. FDR's support held up best in the more internationalist and pro-Allied Northeast and South, and he rolled to overwhelming majorities in Polish and Jewish areas. But the war by no means dominated the electorate's concerns or decisions. War and foreign policy ranked low among the reasons voters gave for favoring Roosevelt or Willkie, and the campaign itself seems not to have changed many minds.

Apart from the still "Solid South," where he won nearly three-fourths of the vote, Roosevelt's most impressive strength lay in the big cities. Cities of more than 100,000, which accounted for one-third of the nation's electorate, gave FDR three-fifths of their vote. The urban returns varied relatively little from region to region and divided between the parties almost everywhere at roughly the same economic level. Indeed, because upper-income voters switched much more substantially toward the Republicans than did middle- and lower-income voters, there was in 1940 an even sharper division by socioeconomic status than in 1936.

Yet voting patterns did not fall out precisely or solely along class lines. Not only did party attachments and party switching often stem from policy views unconnected to class or occupational status, but such factors as race, religion, and ethnicity also shaped the vote. In some working-class Polish-American areas, where ethnic and class issues reinforced one another, the president rolled up "astonishing majorities" of 90 percent and more. By contrast, economic concerns prevented urban

German-American and Italian-American voters from defect-
ing in larger numbers to the GOP; only a quarter of the
upper-income Italians who had voted for FDR in 1936 did
so again in 1940, according to one survey, but half the middle-
income and three-fifths of the lower-income Italian voters
remained with the president. The black vote, largely lower income, remained solidly two-to-one for FDR in 1940 despite
growing restiveness about discrimination and segregation in
the armed forces, defense industries, and elsewhere.

Despite the war's impact on American politics in 1940,
what seems most significant are the basic continuities from the
1930s. Although the war raised new issues and influenced voting, the election turned especially on Roosevelt's domestic
record since 1933, and voting patterns were much like those of
the 1930s. Still "that man" to opponents of the New Deal,
FDR remained the "workingman's hero" to millions more.
Security, the dominant concern of the depression decade, remained central in wartime America. To a majority of voters in
1940, Roosevelt symbolized domestic security—jobs and help
if needed; and he represented global security—peace they
hoped, but at least reassuring experience and pro-Allied sentiment. The Democrats' new majority status was thus reaffirmed in 1940, as were the strength and contours of the
Roosevelt coalition. Neither incipient prosperity nor new
wartime issues much deflected American politics from the
patterns of the depression decade.

THE ELECTION OF 1942 AND THE
SEVENTY-EIGHTH CONGRESS

Just after Pearl Harbor, the chairmen of the Republican
and Democratic National Committees exchanged telegrams
that the Democrats said established "the most complete adjournment of domestic politics since the formation of the two-

party systems." The adjournment proved chimerical. In January 1942 Democratic chairman Edward J. Flynn accused the GOP of being more interested in winning the House of Representatives than in winning the war. He claimed that only a major defeat in battle would harm the nation as much as a Republican Congress. Responding that Flynn wanted to liquidate the GOP, Republican chairman Joseph W. Martin insisted upon the need for vigorous political debate. Partisan politics would continue much as usual in wartime America.

With the United States at war, World War II shaped politics in 1942 more than it had two years before—all the more because it was apparently not going well on the battlefronts or the home front. Americans were not frightened in 1942, but they were frustrated and impatient about the course of the war abroad and about seeming mismanagement at home. In fact 1942 turned out to be the year that set the Allies on the road to victory, but the significance of the battles of the Coral Sea and Midway in the Pacific was not widely recognized at first, while news of the North African invasion and of success at Guadalcanal did not come until after the election. Nor were the outcome of the battle of Stalingrad and the ravages of the Russian front on the German military yet apparent.

At home, production bottlenecks, shortages, rationing, inflation, and confusion and red tape in Washington all seemed part of an inadequate war effort. By late 1942 the war mobilization agencies had begun to sort things out, but successes at home, like victories abroad, still seemed outweighed by difficulties. The Office of Price Administration (OPA), with its price-control and rationing programs, was a particular source of resentment. Pledging to prosecute the war more vigorously and to bring more effectiveness and equity to war mobilization measures, Republicans throughout the nation made the conduct of the war their paramount issue in the 1942 election. They threw the Democrats on the defensive and undercut the obvious Democratic tactic of calling for patriotic unity and support of the president and his party.

Election day brought surprisingly large gains for the GOP. With Republicans gaining almost four dozen additional representatives and nine senators, the new House would be just 218 to 208 Democratic, the Senate 58 to 37. Not only Republicans but also conservative Southern Democrats would have more weight on Capitol Hill because Democratic setbacks came especially among relatively liberal candidates in the Northeast and Midwest. Thus while Democrats retained nominal partisan control of Congress, ideological control, particularly in the House, fell in 1943 and 1944 to a much-enlarged conservative coalition of Republicans and anti–New Deal Democrats.

Dissatisfaction with the war effort at home and abroad seemed at first the obvious reason for the results. Wartime prosperity and the virtual abstention of FDR—"too damn busy being President" to do much politicking, he said—obviously diminished the salience of New Deal issues. Beyond that, a variety of local issues and group grievances—Italian Americans continued to defect disproportionately from the Democratic coalition, for example—further contributed to Republican gains. But two other lines of explanation quickly surfaced and provided important perspectives for understanding the 1942 election.

For one thing, conservative spokesmen and newspapers tended to see the election, in the words of U.S. News, as "a wave of resurgence" against the New Deal. By contrast the New Republic acknowledged that the election was a "disaster" but claimed, like liberals generally, that it was "nonsense" to see in the returns a real Republican or conservative resurgence, for the large philosophical issues were eclipsed by the war and a host of local, petty, and transitory grievances. Liberals had the better part of the electoral analysis, for Republicans had not waged an anti–New Deal campaign in 1942, nor by all evidence can the shift in the vote be ascribed to ideology; but conservatives were right in understanding that voters had sent to Washington a much larger contingent of anti–New Deal Republicans.

The role of voter turnout was the other important focus of discussion. Only 28 million people voted in 1942 as compared with 50 million in 1940. Soon after the election the pollster George Gallup identified the low voter turnout as the most important feature of the election. Because the great majority of nonvoters—young servicemen and migrating war workers especially—were Democrats, he said, the low turnout had produced Republican gains. Buttressed by other analysts, Gallup's explanation soon became a standard interpretation of the election.

But low turnout seems not to have been so central to the 1942 results. Believing that voter apathy and ideological concerns were secondary factors, candidates of both parties said that dissatisfaction with the conduct of the war and with rationing and home-front economic management had been the fundamental reasons for Republican gains, with OPA the major target of voter ire. Opinion polls generally were consistent with that analysis. And there was in any event a significant amount of Democratic-to-Republican voter switching in 1942. A close statistical study of voting in Connecticut—on the surface a clear example of low turnout and sweeping Democratic losses in 1942—found that turnout played a small role in the outcome.

The wartime frustrations and irritations that had roiled the home front all year were the chief reason for the Republican gains. They helped to erode Democratic strength and reveal the vulnerability of the Democratic majority to new circumstances and new issues. Still, voting patterns, with their geographic, socioeconomic, and ethnic cleavages, remained much like those of the previous New Deal–era elections, and the results reflected no great conversion to conservative or anti–New Deal views. Temporarily at least, the war had augmented Republican strength, but it had not brought fundamental change to electoral politics.

The Seventy-eighth Congress nonetheless promised to be the most conservative since the 1920s. Power would be in the hands of what *Fortune* magazine called "normalcy men," many of whom "think they have a mandate to repeal all New Deal reforms." *Time* said Congress was in "open revolt" against the administration and the New Deal; and especially on domestic and postwar issues the new Congress was ready to challenge the executive branch and to assert its own power and influence. As wartime government inevitably grew larger and more powerful, conservatives became even more suspicious of Roosevelt and eager to pare back the regulatory-welfare state. The anti–New Deal, antiexecutive, antiplanning, antispending, antiwelfare, and antistatist animus of Republicans and conservatives, smoldering for ten years and more active since the late 1930s, seemed ready to erupt in the Seventy-eighth Congress. The war had created neither those concerns nor indeed the conservative coalition that would pursue them; but it had intensified sentiments and enlarged the coalition.

In part, congressional conservatives vented their animus by rolling back or terminating a number of relatively minor New Deal agencies. They focused especially on relief agencies that seemed unnecessary during wartime prosperity and that had small or politically weak clienteles. The Seventy-seventh Congress had begun the campaign by cutting off money to the Civilian Conservation Corps (CCC) and attacking the Works Progress Administration (WPA). Although FDR, with other liberals, preferred giving the WPA a "wartime furlough," his energies were focused on the war and he could count the votes on Capitol Hill; accordingly he acceded to Congress by giving the WPA an "honorable discharge" late in 1942. Then in 1943 the Seventy-eighth Congress ended the National Youth Administration (NYA)—like the CCC and WPA now serving especially African Americans and other workers slow to be hired—and crippled the Farm Security Administration (FSA) and the Rural Electrification Administration (REA), both of which in different ways provided help to small and marginal farmers.

Although Congress did not seek to end programs serving large and politically powerful groups—Social Security, the Wagner Act, banking regulation, farm price supports—it revealed its disposition in other ways. Reflecting the political power of commercial farmers, the ceiling on farm prices was allowed to rise; reflecting the clout of big business, industrial demobilization policy focused more on business than on labor and the "human side of reconversion," and tended to favor big business over small in reconversion, contract termination, and surplus property disposal. By contrast, Congress systematically headed off efforts, such as the unsuccessful 1943 Wagner-Murray-Dingell Bill, to expand social insurance, and with the 1943 Smith-Connally Act amended the 1935 Wagner Act in a way that regulated and restricted unions and foreshadowed the postwar Taft-Hartley Act. In 1943 Congress also rejected FDR's cap on salaries and all but killed the domestic branch of the Office of War Information (which conservatives thought merely provided New Deal propaganda). Then in 1944 it passed over an angry FDR's veto a tax bill he regarded as a regressive gift to business and the wealthy. In another effort led by anti–New Deal conservatives, the House Un-American Activities Committee investigated alleged radicals in FDR's administration.

In two areas of postwar policymaking, Congress again revealed both its own preferences and the gradients of power and public opinion in mid-war America. In 1943 it terminated the National Resources Planning Board (NRPB), the principal agency that was developing the liberal Keynesian postwar program for full-employment prosperity, rising standards of living, and economic security. Earlier in the year the NRPB had released two landmark reports, *Security, Work, and Relief Policies* and, even more important, *Post-War Plan and Program,* which called, among other things, for a "new [economic] bill of rights" to include decent jobs, housing, food, recreation, social insurance, and medical care. Proposing much of the postwar liberal agenda not enacted until the mid-1960s, *Post-War Plan and Program* horrified congressional conservatives, opposed as they were to federal planning, spending, and social programs. They reacted not just by burying the report but by liquidating the NRPB.

Refusing even to consider an economic bill of rights, the Seventy-eighth Congress in 1944 did pass the famous GI Bill of Rights. But while the GI Bill shared some of the aims of the NRPB postwar vision—indeed stemmed in part from NRPB proposals—it was passed as reward, not reform, and reflected the enormous political power of veterans and their families, friends, and admirers. It turned out to be one of the landmark pieces of legislation in mid-twentieth-century America. Providing educational benefits and low-interest loans for home ownership, business, and farming, the GI Bill underwrote both prosperity and upward mobility in the postwar era.

In its different actions on the two bills of rights, indeed in its entire agenda, the Seventy-eighth Congress not only demonstrated its own aims and priorities but also largely reflected the public mood. New Deal programs from the 1930s that seemed unnecessary during wartime prosperity and affected relatively few people were cut back or killed. Apart from the special case of the GI Bill, major new proposals for reform and security had no chance. Unions had irritated much of the public with their demands and work stoppages and seemed to deserve sanctions; business, producing the miracles of mobilization that had licked the depression and were winning the war, had regained public esteem and seemed to merit assistance. And surely the GIs deserved what a grateful nation might provide, particularly when help for the veterans involved keys to individual opportunity and middle-class status rather than comprehensive social provision.

Still, for all the power of the conservative coalition and its success against the liberal White House, two other things, reaffirmed by the politics of 1944, should be noted. First, the heart of the New Deal regulatory-welfare state was not rescinded, or even seriously assaulted; all but the most zealous conservatives understood that such a course was likely political suicide. Second, despite the termination of the NRPB and the burial of its postwar program, the liberal Keynesian aim of full-employment prosperity was shared by the public across the political spectrum, and even many conservatives and businessmen understood the importance of fiscal policy to the economy's performance. Although the complete liberal postwar program had no chance for success in the politics of midwar America, its focus on jobs fit exactly the postwar anxieties and priorities of the American people.

THE ELECTION OF 1944

At a famous late 1943 press conference, Franklin D. Roosevelt suggested that "Dr. New Deal" had stepped aside for "Dr. Win-the-War." Seeming to represent at once FDR's wartime priorities, his understanding that the Seventy-eighth Congress was obdurately opposed to reform, and the ebbing of liberal strength in wartime America, Roosevelt's colorful language has long served as a symbol of liberal decline and conservative resurgence during the war. But FDR's meaning was at least in some respects misconstrued. To be sure, his attention was mostly on the war, not on domestic programs or politics; and certainly Congress was firmly controlled by the conservative coalition. But the new liberal Keynesian program had continued to develop during the war, and Roosevelt had not necessarily lost his taste for reform—especially if it was also politically possible and profitable.

In that same press conference the president spoke of the need for a "new program" when the war ended, to "plan for, and help to bring about, an expanded economy which will result in more security, in more employment, in more recreation, in more education, in more health, in better housing for all of our citizens. . . ." If that sounded rather like the NRPB postwar program, FDR's 1944 State of the Union address just two weeks later was even more explicit. He declared his support for "a second Bill of Rights under which a new basis of security and prosperity can be established for all." So important did he consider his address that he insisted on reading it on national radio even though he was too ill to deliver it in person to Congress. In it he emphasized the "economic bill of rights" that would ensure jobs, income adequate for decent homes, food, medical care, and recreation, and social insurance for those without jobs or sufficient income.

Roosevelt's avowal of an economic bill of rights came after pressure from liberals who wanted him to push harder on domestic issues and to lay groundwork for the upcoming presidential election. Throughout the war Eleanor Roosevelt had remained an insistent and important voice, in public and in the White House, for social and economic reform. But during the first half of 1944 the president himself continued to focus on the war and wartime diplomacy and gave relatively little attention to domestic policy and politics. Roosevelt's course of action, which both worried and frustrated many liberals, was consistent with his wartime emphasis on victory in the war above all else.

But the president's apparent inattention to home-front politics no doubt reflected his failing health and energies as well as his wartime priorities. Weakened by the flu in the winter of 1943–1944, he was found during a thorough physical examination in March to suffer from serious hypertension and cardiac disease. Roosevelt was an old, infirm, increasingly gaunt sixty-two in 1944, with even his fabled good cheer ebbing, at least in private. But he repeatedly rallied, retained the serene confidence that had marked his presidency from the beginning, and could usually put on a reassuring public display. The true state of his health was a closely held secret. Perhaps even Roosevelt himself, used to physical difficulties and always persevering, never really knew—or would allow himself to admit—the extent of his debilities.

But if FDR himself rationed little time to politics during the first half of 1944, partisan battles continued apace. One dustup came in Congress over the issue of the service vote in 1944. With some eleven million people in the armed forces in 1944, more than half of them abroad, the service vote promised to be important—and the conventional wisdom, supported by the polls, was that for a variety of reasons GIs were strongly Democratic. Democrats thus wanted to make it as easy as possible for them to vote by federal ballot while Republicans, emphasizing procedural safeguards and states' rights, raised obstacles. Southern Democrats had their own fears that federal ballots would enable blacks to vote, so on this issue too the conservative coalition of Republicans and Southern Democrats found common cause. After months of wrangling in 1943 and early 1944, a middle ground was found that provided state controls but in most areas produced relatively easy procedures enabling soldiers to vote by absentee ballot— as more than four million did.

Meanwhile both parties experienced internal struggles on the way to the fall campaign. Since it seemed obvious that

Roosevelt would seek reelection, the major choices to be made involved who would run against FDR for the Republicans and who would run with FDR for the Democrats. Wendell Willkie, the 1940 GOP nominee, had by 1944 alienated party leaders and rank-and-file Republicans alike with his increasingly liberal views on foreign and domestic policy. Badly defeated in a key primary in Wisconsin, he withdrew from the race, and the Republican nomination went to New York's young governor Thomas E. Dewey. Dewey represented the Eastern wing of the GOP that endorsed responsible postwar internationalism and had come to terms with the lineaments of the New Deal. As in 1940, as indeed even in 1942 and the Seventy-eighth Congress, the GOP platform and campaign indicated that the core of the New Deal was beyond partisan attack. But Dewey and other Republicans did take issue with what they saw as the excesses of the New Deal and big government, and maintained that Republican emphasis on limited government and private enterprise was the way to postwar prosperity.

Democrats had to decide on a running mate for Roosevelt. Having grudgingly acquiesced in the nomination of Henry A. Wallace in 1940, party leaders by 1944 were increasingly unhappy with him. A leading advocate of thoroughgoing social and economic reform at home and a sort of global New Deal abroad, Wallace was too liberal for moderate and conservative Democrats, and he seemed too impolitic and impractical, even too eccentric, for organization regulars. His popularity among liberal Democrats was not sufficient to safeguard his position. The other leading candidate was James F. Byrnes, FDR's "assistant president" for economic policy, with his extraordinary record as a Supreme Court justice and an influential senator in the 1930s. But Byrnes, a conservative South Carolinian, was unpopular among labor, liberals, and blacks, and he had apparent liabilities with the Catholic ethnic vote because he had left the Catholic church.

Roosevelt made no real attempt to salvage Wallace or promote Byrnes, and with his approval the vice-presidential nomination fell to Missouri senator Harry S. Truman. Truman had made a name for himself heading a Senate committee scrutinizing the wartime economic mobilization program, but he was selected not so much for his record or talent as because he fit the Democrats' political needs in 1944. A reliable but moderate New Dealer, he could find support in both the party's liberal and conservative wings. From the border state of Missouri, he seemed able to bridge the party's growing sectional chasm between North and South. A practical politician experienced in dealing with his state's Democratic machine, he was acceptable to party regulars. And he had proved an effective campaigner with the common touch. Both parties thus rebuffed candidates who seemed too liberal on foreign and domestic policy, replacing them with more moderate men whose views were safely within the party and national consensus.

Polls, more important to politicians and political tactics in 1944 than ever before, showed that three issues especially concerned the public: winning the war, ensuring postwar prosperity, and keeping the peace. Among these, postwar prosperity was easily the most important. By the fall of 1944 the end of the war was in sight, with Germany and Japan both in retreat before far more powerful Allied forces. Neither the conduct nor the outcome of the war thus figured significantly in the 1944 campaign, though FDR's candidacy was enhanced by his wartime leadership. Postwar foreign policy was a concern but for most people clearly a secondary one. Roosevelt and Dewey both supported the proposed United Nations, though polls showed that the public had more confidence in Roosevelt to keep the peace.

The overriding public concern, far outweighing the others in opinion surveys, was postwar prosperity, jobs in particular. On that count too the polls showed Roosevelt and the Democrats with a significant lead in public estimation. Again in 1944, politics turned on security, domestic economic security especially; and the presidential election thus pivoted again on Roosevelt, his conduct of the presidency since 1933, and his domestic record and his image as the champion of the common man and of economic security. The politics of 1944 had powerful continuities from the two preceding presidential elections.

New and different issues did arise, to be sure, some of them reflecting the impact of the war. Roosevelt, for example, took pains to placate Polish-American voters, concerned about Soviet intentions in postwar Poland and the future of their homeland. Democrats warned against changing presidents before the war was over and against entrusting global affairs to the young and inexperienced Dewey. Both parties tried to reassure the public about postwar foreign policy.

For their part, Republicans tried two initiatives that led FDR to regard the campaign against him as the meanest of his life. Portraying Roosevelt as old and tired (Dewey was just forty-two), and unable to lead a quarreling, inefficient administration, they emphasized Dewey's youthfulness and energy and warned against a fourth term. Republicans circulated photographs of FDR looking especially old and haggard and spread rumors that went beyond the truth—just as did Democratic reassurances about the president's health. In a brilliant and combative nationally broadcast speech at a labor union dinner, Roosevelt responded to Republican charges and did much to deflect the issue of his age and health. In any event, Dewey's youthfulness had liabilities as well, and he never came across as an engaging, sympathetic person with a feel for ordinary people and their problems; in 1944, as in his famous loss to Truman in 1948, his demeanor and personality detracted from his appeal.

Dewey and his running mate, conservative Ohio governor John W. Bricker, also pushed charges of communism in ways that alarmed some Democrats and earned Roosevelt's contempt. Since the 1930s conservatives had accused Roosevelt and the New Deal of radical un-American tendencies and worse, and in 1940 had hurled charges of both communism and fascism at the administration. In 1944 Republicans warned about softness toward communism abroad and at home. Abroad, the fate of Eastern Europe and what seemed to critics Roosevelt's complicity in Soviet expansion focused Republican charges. At home, Bricker said, "the forces of Communism linked with irreligion . . . are worming their way into our national life," and "are attempting to take a strangle hold on our nation through the control of the New Deal." Dewey too claimed that Communists were taking over the Democratic party under Roosevelt.

Organized labor provided a focus for GOP attacks. Following the 1942 elections and the 1943 Smith-Connally Act, the CIO had formed a Political Action Committee (PAC) to counter antilabor efforts and to get out the working-class vote in 1944. The committee worked closely with Democratic organizations and candidates. Claiming that radical elements, especially in the CIO, were seeking to take over the Democratic party and the nation, some Republicans said that PAC really meant "Party of American Communism." Not a new issue in 1944, Republican charges of radicalism and communism were more intense than before and anticipated the postwar politics of anticommunism. But while preelection polls suggested that the Republican tactic would have bite, postelection surveys proved it largely toothless—at least in 1944.

The campaign, like public concerns, always came back to domestic policy and the central issues of how to ensure full-

employment prosperity and economic security. From the outset Dewey called full employment "a first objective of national
policy" and said that the New Deal had been rescued by the
war but could not ensure postwar jobs and prosperity. Pushed
throughout the year by liberal Democrats to make a stand on
the liberal postwar program, Roosevelt in his final campaign
address returned to themes he had sounded earlier. In what
presidential speechwriter Samuel I. Rosenman termed a "complete statement of the New Deal of 1944," FDR called for the
economic bill of rights—including rights to a job, adequate
income, a decent home, health and medical care, education,
and social insurance. Looking ahead to what he called "the
America of tomorrow," the president envisioned a full-
employment economy with a breathtaking 60 million jobs. (At
the wartime peak there were some 55 million civilian jobs.)
Having dismissed Willkie's 1940 claims about the enormous
potential of the American economy as "a mirage of an island
of dreams," Roosevelt now talked about "this land of unlim-
ited opportunity" where government and business working
together would provide not just jobs but new homes, automobiles, airplanes, and other fruits of an expanding high-
consumption economy of abundance. The booming wartime
economy and the new liberal Keynesian program had taken
FDR and many other liberals from their focus on security and
scarcity in the 1930s to a vision of expansion and abundance in
1944 and beyond.

But as in 1940, so in 1944, the electorate paid more attention
to past records and immediate priorities than to visions of the
future. "Depression psychosis" seemed on its way back, with a
growing concern about postwar jobs and a widespread conviction that government must play a large role in prosperity and
security. Accordingly, voters elected Roosevelt, the symbol of
security and the apparent architect of the dual victory over the
Axis and the depression, to a fourth term. FDR's margin was

down slightly, to thirty-six states and 53.5 percent of the vote; but it was a handsome victory nonetheless. Democrats gained twenty-four seats in the House and lost but two in the Senate.

Voting patterns were remarkably consistent with previous New Deal elections. Indeed, there was less change from 1940 to 1944 than in any pair of elections in the Roosevelt-Truman era, as nearly nine of ten voters cast their ballots as they had in 1940. The urban vote was again critical to the Democratic triumph, and Roosevelt and the Democrats again did best among lower- and middle-income voters, blue-collar workers, Catholic and Jewish ethnic groups, and blacks. In 1944 the hemorrhage of Italian and German voters was stanched, and significant defections of Polish Americans from the Roosevelt coalition failed to materialize. Dewey and the Republicans again did best in the Midwest and among old-stock, Protestant, and better-off voters.

Democrats also easily carried the South again, though with reduced support from apprehensive white Southerners. The 1944 presidential election turned out in fact to be the last for the old Democratic Solid South. Although New Deal liberalism helped to account for Democratic difficulties in the South, it was especially racial concerns, intensified by the war, that in 1944 loosened the Democratic grip on the South. Continuing after the war, racial and ideological concerns turned white Southerners away from the Democratic party in growing numbers. In this way the war certainly contributed to a landmark change in national politics, though prewar trends and especially postwar developments were crucial to the process.

The war had changed salient issues and voting patterns in other ways as well. Foreign and defense policy became issues as they had not been in the 1930s and would remain central to policymaking and often to politics in the postwar era. Roosevelt's image as the successful commander-in-chief was surely instrumental in his 1944 victory. Republican charges of

communism anticipated a powerful postwar issue, though by
1944 Republicans had accused the New Deal of being radical
and un-American for a decade. New ethnic concerns, foreign
policy issues, the return of prosperity, more powerful and
combative conservatism—all these and more had both affected politics and eroded the Democratic majority and the
Roosevelt coalition.

Yet wartime politics were in fundamental ways strikingly
like those of the 1930s. Domestic party issues and images from
the depression decade dominated during the war, and voting
patterns were remarkably consistent with those of the 1930s.
In 1944 Democrats still seemed the party of prosperity and the
common man—above all still the party of Franklin D. Roosevelt, champion campaigner and symbol of security. Politics
reflect the culture, and despite the war's impact, wartime
America and its politics reflected profound continuities from
the past. As one study of the election has put it, "... the 1944
results were almost exactly the same as in 1940 primarily because the political structure of the country remained fixed
during the war." The Roosevelt coalition, forged in the depression and tested in war, had prevailed again.

The politics of wartime America were thus substantially
"politics as usual." Not only did sharp partisanship and the
regular cycles of American elections continue during global
war, but so too did prewar voting patterns and dynamics
of domestic policymaking. The New Deal emerged from the
war essentially intact, as did the Roosevelt coalition and the
Democratic majority, though all were a bit frayed. The congressional conservative coalition, coalescing in the late 1930s,
had grown more powerful, pruning the New Deal on the
margins and preventing its significant extension, while prosperity, foreign affairs, and traditional conservative antistatism
had whittled the Democratic majority. But the ideological, in-

stitutional, and political constraints on the New Deal antedated the war years. World War II was no watershed in
American politics, nor did it produce an elevated politics of
nonpartisan unity.

8

Glimpses of War, Visions of Peace

THE UNITED STATES largely escaped the terrible ravages of World War II. Worldwide the war cost an estimated 15 million to 20 million military dead and missing, 40 million to 60 million civilian dead and missing, and countless more wounded or injured. The Soviet Union alone suffered 20 million to 25 million deaths. Much of Europe and Japan was reduced to rubble, with tens of millions homeless or displaced. By contrast, the continental United States never experienced battle or destruction, and the nation lost some 292,000 combat dead and another 114,000 military deaths from other causes—tragedies for them and their families, but a fraction of the human toll elsewhere.

Most Americans thus had only glimpses of the war, viewed largely through the censored and often distorting filters of photos and newsreels, newspaper and radio reports, movies, and letters home. To home-front Americans, combat could seem more glorious and ennobling than it was, even though like the GIs they chiefly sought victory and the end of the war rather than having some lofty sense of war aims or global mission. Visions of peace focused especially on home, family, jobs, and the good life of abundance and security denied for the fifteen long years of depression and war. Just as wartime Americans often resisted home-front change, so most of them wanted a postwar future that was essentially a more prosperous and secure version of the past.

SCENES OF BATTLE

Residual images of GI Joe and his experiences are often as inaccurate as those of Rosie the Riveter. If most wartime women did not go to work, most wartime men did not go to war. To be sure, two of every three males aged seventeen to thirty-five served in the armed forces during World War II. But that was just one-third of all adult males; and of the sixteen million who did enter the military, one-fourth never left the United States, and only a minority of GIs who went overseas served in actual combat areas. Deferments for key industrial and agricultural workers, for college students, and until the middle of the war for fathers; rejections for a variety of physical and mental reasons; and even some draft evasion all helped shape the armed forces.

Emphasizing the everyday traditional virtues of the American GI, reporters often embellished the degree to which the nation's fighting men came out of the small towns and farms and playing fields of the American home front—newsboys and older brothers and hometown heroes off to war. Such people there were in the military, but they were joined by GIs from urban slums, from the hollows of Appalachia, from various minority groups, and from privileged backgrounds and enclaves too. Government efforts to portray a diverse and democratic "people's army" were thus close to the mark, though they usually ignored or obscured the stratifications and tensions also present in the armed forces.

Despite the selection process and motivational efforts, GIs (like home-front Americans) often had little sense of the ideological character of the war. Only 13 percent could name three of the "Four Freedoms" that FDR had declared as the nation's

war aims—freedom of speech and religion, freedom from
want and fear—while one-third could name none. Studies indicated that just one in twenty GIs fought for such clear idealistic reasons as the threat to democracy. They fought instead to
support their buddies and their units, to avoid shame or sanctions, to get revenge, especially for Pearl Harbor. They fought
above all to win and return home.

John Hersey, a war correspondent who wrote a classic account of the atomic bombing of Hiroshima, understood the
GIs' war aims. When he asked marines at Guadalcanal what
they were fighting for, no one spoke at first and then one
whispered, clearly for all of them, "Jesus, what I'd give for a
piece of blueberry pie." On reflection, Hersey recognized that
fighting for pie was "not exactly what they meant . . . here pie
was their symbol for home." They were fighting, he knew,
"'to get the goddam thing over and get home.'" And as he
knew too, ". . . home seems to most marines a pretty good
thing to be fighting for. Home is where the good things are—
the generosity, the good pay, the comforts, the democracy, the
pie."

By contrast, the motivational instruction and indoctrination
was, so it seemed often to the GIs, the "bullshit" they had to
listen to as they did their duty and sought their own war aims
and meanings. And if servicemen resisted the "bullshit" of official rhetoric and indoctrination, so they resented the "chick-
enshit" of military life—the rules and regulations that were so
often petty, irrelevant, even incomprehensible, and the small-
minded authoritarianism and self-promotion of too many officers. GIs derided public relations efforts that produced the
sanitized, glorified, and distorted versions of the war shown in
movies and the media. Even in combat zones the military experience typically was one of long stretches of boredom and
anxiety, alleviated as possible by letters and reading material
from home, booze, women, and camaraderie, and punctuated

by the horrific brutality and carnage of combat. Along with comic books, advertisements depicting the good life of traditional values and new abundance were among the favorite reading matter of American servicemen. The "real war," whether the drinking and escapism or the savagery and fear, rarely got into print, photos, or films.

And that real war could be an awful experience indeed. Equipment failed, officers made disastrous mistakes, the enemy seemed relentless, the environment, especially in the Pacific, was not just hostile and debilitating but sometimes deadly. Casualties mounted sharply in the last year of the war as American forces pushed the Germans and the Japanese back. In addition to the toll in dead and wounded, American GIs experienced much higher rates than reported or remembered (up to a fifth or more of hospitalizations) of "neuropsychiatric" cases—combat fatigue, or what was called "shell shock" in World War I and more recently "post-traumatic stress syndrome." On the other hand, new drugs and practices made World War II medical care enormously better than in previous wars, both in saving lives and returning GIs to service. The war was a turning point in military medicine, with large implications for postwar medical care.

Home-front views of the war often differed sharply from battlefield realities. The armed forces kept what was termed their "Chamber of Horrors"—photographs that they would not release for publication because they seemed too grisly or otherwise inappropriate. Not until 1943 were photos of dead Americans released for publication; not until 1945 did *Life* show American blood being shed; and images of mental breakdowns were routinely withheld. The rhythm of the release of combat photographs and films was shaped by propaganda and morale considerations. Before 1943 and the clear turn of the tide it was regarded as harmful to morale to show pictures of dead Americans; once the Allies were successfully on the offensive, government officials feared overconfidence and a slackening of the war effort and released sanitized photographs of American dead in order to motivate home-front Americans.

Much of the control of images and information was simple decency and good taste—not showing the faces of dead or badly injured men, for example, or not releasing the most gruesome photographs of broken and mutilated bodies or of men experiencing mental breakdowns. Much of it was voluntary, out of a sense of common cause and also a desire to avert more heavy-handed government controls. Reporters and news broadcasters were given more leeway than photographers and cameramen, evidently on the grounds that words had less emotional impact than images and were harder to censor—though press accounts were also vetted by the government, and journalists willingly protected sensitive information. And American censorship was in any event less coercive and extreme than in the other belligerent nations.

Still, whether forced or voluntary—and the story was often a complicated interplay of the two—censorship and the control of information shaped perceptions of the war. The armed forces also had their own accomplished and frequently heroic photo and film crews, whose releases were similarly subject to review and censorship—and that were often used for public relations purposes, not only to glorify individual leaders but also to provide favorable publicity and build public support for the different branches of the armed forces. But whatever the motives, the real war was scarcely glimpsed in films, newspapers, and magazines, nor were the social tensions and occasional outbreaks of violence in the military, nor the rates of venereal disease and alcohol use, nor the mental breakdowns. The experience of combat was more brutal and savage, its physical and mental impact larger and more lasting, than myth and memory would have it.

Nor, after the war, were veterans always welcomed as warmly or their readjustments as happy as memories of the Good War suggest. Many at home feared that hardened and jobless veterans would threaten postwar social and political stability. Some veterans did indeed have trouble adjusting to civilian lives, while uncounted others suffered from posttraumatic stress syndrome that produced alcoholism, family troubles, and economic difficulties. In many instances the father's return to families whose members and dynamics had changed was more disturbing than the parting and separation. And for years and decades after the war, Veterans' Administration hospitals dealt with the physical and psychic scars of combat.

But if many home-front Americans worried about the adjustment of the veterans and some even feared them as a disruptive influence, the great majority welcomed and honored them and helped them as they could. If significant numbers of veterans had persisting postwar problems, most adjusted at least satisfactorily. Partly because of their wartime experience, millions enjoyed postwar success far beyond their prewar expectations. Half the veterans received education or training benefits, many of them college educations, changing their lives and American society and changing American higher education as well. In 1947 half of all college students were veterans. With one-fifth of all new homes from the mid-1940s until the mid-1960s financed by the GI Bill, veterans' benefits also fueled the postwar housing boom and became another force for change and mobility in American life. Providing medical and pension payments as well, veterans' benefits became the most expensive piece of social legislation in the budget— by 1950 nearly one-third of social welfare spending. For most GIs, World War II had an important and generally salutary impact on their lives—and through them on the nation. The leadership of World War II servicemen in postwar poli-

tics, including every president from Dwight Eisenhower to
George Bush, is but one evidence of that.

INFORMATION AND IMAGES

Partly because of memories of World War I excesses, President Roosevelt was from the beginning wary of government
censorship and propaganda, reluctant to impose stringent controls. In 1941 he rejected what he termed a "wild scheme"
from the armed forces for "complete censorship of publications, radio, and motion pictures within the U.S.A." But committed to victory above all and understanding the need for
military secrets and public morale, FDR also recognized the
potential importance of controlling information. He said pri-
vately, "I am perfectly willing to mislead and tell untruths if it
will help us win the war."

Although more often deceptive than deceitful, the administration from the start took steps to channel information and
shape perceptions of the war and wartime America. When
earlier agencies proved inadequate to the task, Roosevelt in
October 1941 established the Office of Facts and Figures
(OFF) to coordinate information on national defense. Explicitly devoted to the "strategy of truth," OFF veered toward
what one journalist called "propaganda *for* the truth" in order
to convey its intended messages. But limited in power and disturbed by what it saw as distortions of information by the
press and politicians, OFF met with more frustration than
success.

The apparent need for a more powerful and effective
agency led Roosevelt to create the Office of War Information
(OWI) in June 1942. Headed by the respected CBS radio news
broadcaster Elmer Davis, OWI was expected to coordinate
the dissemination of war information by all federal agencies
and to "formulate and carry out, through the use of press,

radio, motion picture, and other facilities, information programs designed to facilitate the development of an informed and intelligent understanding, at home and abroad, of the status and progress of the war effort and of the war policies, activities, and aims of the Government." As with OFF, information was important, but understandings were essential. A separate Office of Censorship, headed by Associated Press news editor Byron Price, had authority over incoming and outgoing international communications, including film, that did not fall under military censorship.

OWI's principal message, in the words of Elmer Davis, was "that we are coming, that we are going to win, and that in the long run everybody will be better off because we won." Accordingly the agency in all its diverse operations—which included withholding and disseminating information, producing films and radio broadcasts, publishing leaflets, pamphlets, and magazines, monitoring Hollywood films, coordinating government propaganda and public relations efforts—sought to display not just the war effort but American society and culture in the most positive ways. OWI publicized the liberal principles of the 1941 Atlantic Charter (agreed to by Roosevelt and Churchill) and the Four Freedoms as the nation's war aims. It also promoted favorable views of the nation that sought those aims and of a decent, tolerant, diverse, and democratic people, idealistic but tough and practical, working together in common cause toward victory and a just peace. Sometimes admitting flaws in American life—in race relations and in socioeconomic disparities, for example—OWI minimized them and emphasized that such problems were being addressed and solved.

In publicizing the nation's purpose and strengths, OWI also lauded the leadership and vision of President Roosevelt. An understandable part of overseas propaganda and even of home-front motivation, such efforts had obvious political overtones as well. The OWI magazine *Victory* went so far as to contrast the New Deal with such "reactionaries" as Herbert Hoover. Not surprisingly, OWI, dominated by liberal writers and bureaucrats, quickly ran into trouble with conservatives and Republicans, who labeled the agency, its domestic branch in particular, part of the effort to reelect FDR for a fourth term. OWI activities on behalf of racial tolerance and change outraged many white Southerners. The conservative Seventy-eighth Congress of 1943–1944 took OWI as one of its targets, and in the summer of 1943 gutted the domestic branch while continuing, under ongoing scrutiny, the foreign branch with its clearer and less controversial overseas mission.

OWI purposefully avoided the excesses of the World War I Committee on Public Information, and government censorship and propaganda fell well short of what occurred in the other nations at war. Like other mobilization agencies, OWI's powers were limited, especially over the military, which only slowly and reluctantly released information that was not positive or self-serving. (The top navy brass, OWI people said, wanted to issue no statements at all until the one declaring victory.) Still, whatever the limits of its power and controls, and whatever the extent of its success in providing information and building support for the war at home and abroad, OWI reflected the government's readiness not only to withhold but also to manipulate information in wartime America.

In pursuing its aims, OWI worked closely with the motion picture industry. Headed by White House assistant Lowell Mellett, OWI's Bureau of Motion Pictures (BMP) produced and distributed its own films, consulted with other government agencies about their films for public release, and advised Hollywood on how it could help the war effort. In addition to Hollywood personnel who worked with mobilization agencies, an estimated one-third of the motion picture industry's male workers entered the armed forces where they helped produce educational and informational films for the military. Movie stars made personal appearances at home and abroad, and both Hollywood and local theaters helped to promote bond drives and Red Cross and USO efforts. Motion picture personnel also cooperated by producing and showing inspirational films, newsreels, and the like in factories, community centers, and movie houses throughout the war. Frank Capra's celebrated "Why We Fight" series made for the War Department but ultimately distributed to civilians was a particularly good example of such connections, as were the short "Victory Films" distributed by the OWI and shown in commercial theaters.

Given their prominence in American culture, feature films seemed especially important in the war effort. Just after Pearl Harbor, Roosevelt called the motion picture "one of our most effective mediums in informing and entertaining our citizens." He said too that films "must remain free insofar as national security will permit. I want no censorship of the motion picture." The BMP's Mellett declared that "freedom of the screen is as important as freedom of press or of speech."

But as World War II enlarged the role of movies as purveyors of meaning and custodians of public memory, inevitable tensions arose between information and entertainment, between freedom and national security. Censorship of various sorts occurred, though typically by means of the velvet glove rather than the mailed fist, typically indeed with Washington and Hollywood hand-in-hand. Hollywood was used to self-censorship because of its own Production Code, wished to avoid precedent-setting explicit and statutory government censorship, worried about antitrust litigation or the denial of material priorities, and fretted perhaps even more about profits, especially if the Office of Censorship denied export privileges when the industry earned some 40 percent of its proceeds abroad. Over and above such calculations was the sense of unity and common cause in wartime America that prompted scientists, academics, businessmen, workers, and ordinary folk as well as Hollywood moguls, actors, and production people to enlist in the war effort. Heavily Jewish at its top levels, Hollywood needed no patriotic cues or government sanctions to support the war against Nazi Germany. It adopted anti-Axis and interventionist themes in films and newsreels well before Pearl Harbor, particularly after Germany (followed by Italy) barred U.S. films from areas under its control in 1940 and concern about those markets no longer inhibited filmmakers.

The chief question that OWI and the government wanted filmmakers to ask was, "Will this picture help win the war?" The answer could be found in such considerations as how far a film contributed "something new to our understanding of the world conflict" and did not "harm the war effort by creating a false picture of America, her allies, or the world we live in." Avoiding either pessimism or excessive optimism, Hollywood, said the OWI, should portray the contributions and sacrifices of the American people working in common cause across lines of class, ethnicity, gender, and even race, and present the correct images of American ideals and war aims, the enemy, the United Nations, war production, home-front life, and the armed forces. OWI and Office of Censorship policy meant that class conflict, racial discrimination, crime, poverty, and other unsavory aspects of American life were not to be part of Hollywood's version of wartime America. Unity, virtue, and ultimate success—these were the fundamental messages films should carry, messages not so different from Hollywood's own Production Code.

The Bureau of Motion Pictures could suggest topics and approaches, but its real authority over Hollywood came in reviewing proposed treatments and scripts "voluntarily" submitted by the studios. The agency reviewed some 1,650 movie scripts, often suggesting changes in dialogue and emphasis, occasionally urging a studio not to produce or release a film. Beyond that the BMP could recommend that the Office of Censorship bar offending films from overseas distribution. When changes were suggested, Hollywood typically complied. Even when the BMP was weakened in 1943 as part of the evisceration of the domestic branch of the OWI, its policies, precedents, and potential penalties shaped feature film content until the end of the war. Profits and propaganda as well as politics continued to shape wartime movies.

Generalizing about the countless films made during World War II is fraught with difficulty, yet some common themes emerged, consistent with other wartime patterns and propaganda efforts. Hollywood portrayals of the armed forces stressed both teamwork and the diversity of the team—on air crews, in foxholes, at shipboard battle stations, "Americans all" bravely fought and vanquished the Axis. Movies depicted valiant Soviet, democratic British, and modernizing Chinese allies prevailing with the Americans over the uniquely treacherous and beastly "Japs" in the Pacific and the brutal Nazis in Europe. Films early in the war tended to avoid the grim side of combat and sometimes came close to being little more than adventure movies. As with photos, so with films, Allied successes by 1943 led the government to urge more realistic combat films to dispel overconfidence and apathy. Similarly, newsreels that had often looked like travelogues in 1942 and 1943 became more graphic in 1944 and 1945.

Even when they sought a certain realism, however, films tended to follow old genres, adapted for the war. As Hollywood's techniques interacted with Washington's purposes, the results were often oversimplified versions of good versus evil and celebrations of American virtue and success. And even when they showed more accurately the nature and impact of the war, films avoided depicting wrenching change in the fabric of American life. Movies that portrayed women going beyond old boundaries in the armed forces or on the home front, for example, were careful not to challenge old norms and to provide images of traditional femininity and women's roles. Government films that depicted black contributions and racial change and sought to build African-American morale tried to avoid upsetting whites with overt criticism or challenges to existing patterns. Working-class Americans received respectful attention, but within the framework of wartime unity and traditional middle-class values and aspirations.

Filmgoers in any event seemed weary of war movies by 1943 and preferred more familiar and escapist fare. Like the combat films, other wartime movies also reflected the continuing hold of old ways and old patterns and reinforced traditional values and self-images. In Hollywood's sentimental and melodramatic approaches, movies confirmed American virtues and celebrated romance, family, hard work, adventure, and the good life of abundance. The images and symbols that wartime Americans found—and sought—in films echoed through postwar American life.

Advertising also served as an arm of government as well as an image-maker for business during the war. Advertisers were volunteers rather than draftees, for the coming of war directly threatened them. Was there a need for advertising when manufacturers either produced war goods for government purchase or found easy markets for consumer goods? Indeed, didn't advertising exacerbate inflationary pressures by raising costs and fueling demand? Would the government eliminate tax write-offs for advertising or prohibit advertising costs in war contracts and price controls? Reflecting the anxieties of advertising agencies about such issues, the War Advertising Council was formed soon after Pearl Harbor in order to find a valued and thus protected place for advertising in wartime America.

The Ad Council worked with the OWI and other government agencies, with advertising agencies and sponsoring businesses, and with the media to coordinate "war advertising." This it defined as advertising "which induces people, through information, understanding, and persuasion to take certain actions necessary to the winning of the war." The council coordinated war bond drives, financed by money and space donated by business, for the Treasury Department. In numerous other ways as well, advertisements helped home-front mobilization, from recruiting men and women for military service and production jobs to supporting scrap metal and fat salvage campaigns, to conserving food and vital materials, to understanding and supporting price controls. In 1942 the Ad Council supported fourteen campaigns for eight government agencies accounting for $150 million in donated time and space; in 1943 the figures were thirty-four campaigns for seventeen agencies at $284 million; in 1944 sixty-two campaigns for twenty-seven agencies at $302 million. Advertisers could, and did, claim they had gone to war—and helped win it.

But despite their public service and the patriotism that informed their efforts, advertisers also went to work for themselves and their clients. The time and space "donated"—thus saving the government money—helped keep advertisers' names before the public, sometimes blatantly and self-servingly so. Polls indicated that the advertising industry specifically and business generally had significantly greater prestige after the war than before it. Expenditures for advertising increased by one-third, from $2.2 billion to $2.9 billion, between 1942 and 1945. And while the Advertising Council claimed that in all more than $1 billion in services had been donated to the war effort, favorable decisions on tax write-offs and advertising expenses cost the government revenue.

But there was another price of using advertising in mobilization: Madison Avenue's portrayal of the war was even further removed than Hollywood's from the "real war" and its meaning. Advertisements portrayed American GIs as innocent idealists, easygoing but dedicated heroes whose courage and ingenuity would bring inevitable victory. Advertising images of the war typically were melodramatic and sentimental, not realistic; they suggested adventure, glory, and success, not the brutality, costs, and uncertainty of combat. Death was distant and abstract, American virtue and victory certain. And ads often implied that by saving some tin, or by buying a bond—or a brand-name product—home-front Americans sacrificed or contributed to victory in ways comparable to the GIs.

Wartime advertisements also produced images of wartime and postwar America that fit the values, hopes, and fears of the American people. Nor should that be surprising, for beyond the obvious interaction between advertising and the culture, advertisers, like politicians and policymakers, by the war years paid more attention to opinion surveys than ever before. Throughout the war advertisers painted reassuring and sentimental pictures of home-front America as a place of sacrifice, hard work, and common cause, where traditional values and patterns of life would sustain the fighting men, themselves products and protectors of a timeless Norman Rockwell America. Images of small-town America, of the corner drugstore, of old-fashioned virtues and folkways—and of Mom's pies—figured prominently in advertising portrayals of wartime America.

The ads carried political as well as cultural messages. Not only American freedom but the American free-enterprise system would forge the sinews of war, preserve the American way, and produce the good life of abundance. In this way too, American might and American right were intertwined, and the American way had to be sustained. In one advertisement an aviator wrote home:

America has come to mean just this to me...a country where I can live the way my folks and I have always lived...a country where there's work to do, where no one is ashamed to work, where there are no limits on a man's ambition or his opportunity to go as far as ability can take him—to grow as great as he wants to be. Whatever you do, don't change that, ever! I know now—*that's* what I'm fighting for!

But if the American way of life would be unchanged, the American standard of living—because of the American way of life—would be enormously better. At the same time the ads of the late war years celebrated unchanging values, virtues, and patterns of life, they also promised the products and abundance of a better life far beyond that of the depression decade. "We have so many things, here in America, that belong only to a free people," said one ad—such things as "Warm, comfortable homes. Automobiles and radios by the million. Electrical machines to keep and cook our food; to wash and clean for us." Advertisements and images, reminiscent of what had seemed the incredible marvels of the future at the 1939–1940 New York World's Fair, now promised technology's bounties by way of new airports, superhighways, wonderful cars, houses full of new electric marvels, indeed a virtual horn of plenty. Taking the very theme of the World's Fair, ads promised "a better, brighter World of Tomorrow."

The emphasis on the good life and the prewar status quo was portrayed perhaps most powerfully in striking advertisements of Nash-Kelvinator in 1944 and 1945. In one of them a somber young blond speaks to her far-off husband:

When you come back to me, you will find nothing changed. Those at home promise that....

Our house still stands, white and lovely as it always was, and down the street the maples march straight and tall,

unwithered by the heat of war! And every Sunday, steeple
bells still ring and in our church we still sing hymns to God.

I've told the children, and I tell myself, this is what
you're fighting for! These are the big and little things
worth waiting for. The things that make our lives worth
living, that make this war worth winning....

Back home to the same town, to the same job you liked
so much...to the same America we have always known
and loved...where you can work and plan and build...
where we and our children are free to make our lives what
we want them to be....

You've said, "That's the America I want when I come
back...don't change that, ever...don't let anyone tamper
with a way of living that works so well."

Never fear, darling—that's the way we *all* want it.

HOME-FRONT ROLES, POSTWAR GOALS

As the ads, the movies, the government, and plain common
sense told wartime Americans, they had to win the war before
they could attain their vision of peace. Most were confident
of victory from the beginning. Pearl Harbor brought shock
and anger and often persistent anxieties, especially about
loved ones; but there was little real fear about the eventual
outcome and much national resolve and confidence. Roosevelt's leadership provided strength and assurance, but so too
did religious faith and the capabilities and efforts of the
American people themselves.

On hearing the news of Pearl Harbor, Don Johnson experienced "an immediate concern—uncertainty, panic," but that
quickly became "indignation, then it turned to anger, and by
the time one went to work the following morning it was determination: 'They can't do this to us.'" William Pefley, who
worked in a Virginia shipyard, said that "Overnight there was
a complete change in attitude....Now it was our war. So

everybody decided, 'No matter what the hours may be, let's get the ships out. Whatever we can do to help this war effort, we are going to do.'"

Americans went to work that morning, and for more than thirteen hundred more, to win the war. But home-front roles went beyond war production. In countless other ways Americans supported the war effort—buying bonds, saving paper, rubber, scrap metal, and fat, doing without new consumer goods and making old ones last longer. Everyone from children to the elderly took part in such campaigns, and helped with the millions of Victory gardens that produced a significant percentage of all vegetables grown. Particularly in the early stages of the war, the Office of Civilian Defense helped to organize local civil defense activities—by early 1942 some 5.6 million people and more than 7,000 local councils took part in such efforts as air-raid defense, coastal surveillance, and blackouts or dimouts. Curfews were sometimes implemented.

Home-front life could be difficult. Shortages affected key consumer durable goods—autos for example—and some foodstuffs. They sometimes caused hardships, like the short supplies of fuel in the cold winter of 1943. Rationing became a necessary but often irritating part of wartime life, as did the hidden inflation of lower quality, diminished choice, reduced services, and inconvenient shopping. Working wives had the often exhausting duties of balancing workplace and home, all the more stressful emotionally when their husbands were off to war. Yet there was also a sense of common cause, of contributing to victory in a just and necessary war. Many found wartime life enormously rewarding, some found it exciting, even exhilarating.

Although much home-front lore has it that Americans gladly sacrificed during the Good War, there was little real sacrifice and a good deal of grousing. "Use it up, wear it out, make it do, or do without," ran the wartime refrain—but there was not much doing without. Production of consumer goods increased during the war, and consumer spending (corrected for inflation) rose by more than 20 percent from 1941 to 1945. On Pearl Harbor Day 1944, Macy's department store in New York City had its biggest sales day ever. In food consumption as in other areas, home-front Americans fared much better than their counterparts among other belligerents. As one example, American per capita meat consumption rose from 134 pounds before the war to 162 pounds by 1944; in Great Britain it fell from 132 pounds to 115 pounds. Despite shortages and rationing, Americans achieved higher nutritional standards than before, with lower-income people making especially notable gains. Besides spending more, people also saved; bank accounts reached record highs, and prewar mortgages and other debts were paid down.

Removed as they were from the battlefronts, prospering during and because of the war, home-front Americans seemed to be fighting the war on "imagination"—an imagination shaped by Washington, Hollywood, and Madison Avenue. In wartime America, in the parlance of economists, making guns for distant combat produced the butter of domestic prosperity. One visitor, struck by the contrasts between the United States and Great Britain, noted that on a pat of butter served him on an airplane was the message REMEMBER PEARL HARBOR. In America, he observed later, "It needed the butter to remind one of the guns." Nor did the Russian, British, German, and Japanese home fronts need the wartime American slogan "Don't you know there's a war on?" to elicit cooperation and explain sacrifice.

Wartime Americans also found ways to enjoy themselves. Movie attendance set new records during the war, rising from 85 million moviegoers per week in 1939 to 95 million per week in 1945 and sending box office receipts from $1 billion to $1.5 billion. In addition to movies, nightclubs, sporting events, and vacations, people also entertained themselves at home, sometimes necessarily so because of travel restrictions, shortages, long work days, and occasional curfews. Radio listening increased sharply, boosted by interest in war news (shaped partly, along with other radio programming, by the OWI's domestic branch). Reading increased too, helped by the growing publication of inexpensive paperbacks. Nonfiction books outsold fiction—war reporter Ernie Pyle was the most popular author—but mysteries sold well and comic book purchases increased spectacularly. Parlor games remained popular, with sales of playing cards increasing by 1,000 percent. Snappy, optimistic, and forgettable war songs appeared early in the war, but nostalgic, sentimental songs looking ahead to home and the end of the war—"White Christmas," "I'll Be Home for Christmas," "I'll Be Seeing You"—appealed more on battlefronts and home front alike. Magazines, comics, songs, movies—all those central features of the popular culture offered glimpses of war and wartime life but provided essentially escapist entertainment and, as the war neared its end in 1944 and 1945, complementary visions of American life and the postwar world.

As Americans at home and abroad thought about what peace would bring, they rarely thought in ideological terms about the war's meaning, about the Four Freedoms and the larger significance that governments and leaders tried to apply to the war. Like John Hersey's marines and the men and women portrayed in wartime ads, they worked and fought for the pie, for home, for comfort. They sought better times ahead for them and their families, not a different world abroad or at home. As *Fortune* magazine said about the GIs, the average American didn't "want a new America. He wants the old one—only more of it."

From the beginning of the war until the end, jobs and economic security were the paramount postwar concern of wartime Americans, the chief benchmark of a good war. And throughout, most Americans were less confident of victory over the Great Depression than of victory over the Axis. A Roper poll on the eve of Pearl Harbor revealed widespread public pessimism about the postwar era despite general confidence that the Axis would be defeated. Of those with an opinion, nearly two-thirds thought there would be "lots of unemployment" and that people would be paid less after the war; indeed, about half of all those surveyed believed that postwar unemployment would match or exceed the worst of the Great Depression. The poll reflected the fears that drove American hopes about the postwar era.

Wartime prosperity reduced but did not dispel "depression psychosis" and the "fear of plenty." Surveys taken in 1942 and 1943 generally showed half or more of Americans still worried about high levels of unemployment and a possible return to depressionlike conditions once the war boom was over, but they also showed increased confidence about postwar circumstances and opportunities. And most of those concerned about general economic conditions after the war were optimistic about their own chances for keeping or getting good jobs. Such attitudes help explain the lack of effective public support for the postwar program released in 1943 by the liberal National Resources Planning Board. While most Americans wanted the New Deal continued, they did not envision a fullblown welfare state and did not want far-reaching new reforms. They preferred jobs and advancement within the existing system.

To some degree, then, the postwar hopes of wartime Americans echoed themes sounded in the advertisements. Like GIs portrayed in the Nash-Kelvinator ads, servicemen, according to one observer, thought "of the United States they left behind as the ultimate in desirability—socially, politically, and every other way. They fight primarily to get the war over so they can return to it as it was, unchanged." So too with home-front Americans. By roughly a two-to-one margin, Americans polled in 1943 said they wanted "the country pretty much the way it was before the war," not significant change or reform. The sentiment persisted through war's end.

But if Americans did not want major reform or large changes in the fabric of American life and government, neither did they wish to return to the pre–New Deal political economy. Even at the height of mid-war optimism, most wanted the core of the New Deal maintained, security protected, employment ensured. And if wartime Americans hoped for—even began to expect—a brighter economic future, they did so cautiously and prudently. They worried, saved, and planned sensible purchases while hoping to afford the cars, houses, and home furnishings and appliances shown in the advertisements.

The politics of 1944 nicely reflected the hopes and fears as well as the decisions and directions of wartime America. In his final major speech of the campaign, calling for a far-reaching economic bill of rights in a full-employment economy, Roosevelt also expansively envisioned a new and better "America of tomorrow." A few days later he said, "I look forward, under the leadership of this Government, to an era of expansion and production and employment. . . . I look forward to millions of new homes, fit for decent living; to new, low-priced automobiles; new highways; new airplanes and airports; to television; and other miraculous new inventions and discoveries, made during this war, which will be adapted to the peacetime uses of a peace-loving people."

FDR's vision of postwar America was in one way much like that of the wartime advertisements. In words closely paralleling Roosevelt's, a GI in an October 1944 ad said, "I see a new America. . . . I see new cities rising up . . . new roads, new homes, new schools . . . new factories that will plan and build

for peace the way they planned and built for war." But in another way, FDR's vision was quite different from that of the
advertisers, for he also spoke for the New Deal mixed economy in which the government had a major role in providing
opportunity, underwriting prosperity, and ensuring security.
Memories of the past shaped public opinion and politics in
1944 more than did visions of the future. Reelected in 1944 less
as the champion of new reform than as the symbol of security
and the nation's leader in the twin victory over the Axis and
the Great Depression, FDR understood, better than the advertisers or his adversaries, the fears as well as the hopes of
wartime Americans. As he had in the depression, the president provided not only leadership but understanding, confidence, and a sense of direction.

In their different ways, Washington, Hollywood, Madison
Avenue, and the American people themselves projected versions of a good war and a good peace. Wartime ideas of a good
war, shaped by the partial glimpses of war afforded by public
and private image-making, were not altogether congruent
with subsequent postwar understandings, but they contained
many of the same elements—a just and necessary war against
evil, waged by a united, virtuous, and democratic people, cul-
minating in victory abroad and prosperity and peace in the
years ahead. Visions of peace were shaped less by propaganda
and images than by long-standing preferences and aspirations
and by the hard experiences of depression and war. The perceptions of war and prescriptions for peace of wartime America, reflecting in part the impact of the war on the nation's
institutions and imagination, resonated powerfully after the
war and helped shape American life and public policy in the
postwar era.

9

Epilogue

WORLD WAR II came to its end in the spring and summer of 1945 with a concatenation of shocking, dismaying, and joyous events. As the Allies pushed into Germany, they found the Nazi death camps, ghastly testimony to the horror of the Holocaust. In April Franklin D. Roosevelt died. Millions of Americans could remember no other president, and millions more could imagine none other than FDR, the familiar and inspiriting personification of the nation's strength and security. In May Germany surrendered, but the celebrations of V-E day were muted not only by the disturbing events earlier in the year but also by the bloody war still being waged in the Pacific. With the defeat of Germany, growing discord between the United States and the Soviet Union threatened to rend the wartime Grand Alliance. In August came the atomic bombing of Hiroshima and Nagasaki, then the surrender of Japan. The war at last was over. Festive celebrations erupted around the country, and the GIs began to return home.

But the jubilation at victory could not suppress forebodings, and not only about the developments of 1945. "Depression psychosis" flared, and contract cancellations and workforce cutbacks gave palpable cause for anxiety, particularly about returning veterans and displaced war workers. Not only the availability of jobs but the end of regular overtime pay and the ratcheting up of prices as controls ended raised concerns about maintaining the wartime standard of living.

The new year seemed no better. Trying to safeguard wartime gains, organized labor in 1946 continued a series of strikes that involved perhaps 10 percent of the workforce and seemingly threatened to paralyze the nation's production and transportation. Sharp inflation, scarce housing, and shortages of consumer goods frustrated and frequently angered the public. Relations with the Soviet Union worsened, and at home the remnants of wartime common cause seemed to evaporate. Trying to cope with postwar problems, Harry Truman, apparently no substitute for FDR, plummeted in the public's estimation. Republicans campaigned in the 1946 midterm elections with the telling slogan "Had Enough?"—and the GOP captured Congress for the first time since the presidency of Herbert Hoover.

But the worst fears of a return to the depression never materialized. Wartime savings, pent-up demand, and speedy reconversion helped the economy turn the corner, and by 1946 peacetime prosperity was well launched. All the while Americans tried to return to a sort of normalcy in their everyday lives. In the fall of 1945 newspapers and magazines carried stories about GI Joe and Rosie the Riveter returning home in their different ways, about the resumption of the college football weekend, about automobile drives and hunting trips and picnics and family reunions—about Americans picking up their old ways of life. But the homecomings and reunions were not unfailingly happy or uncomplicated, nor could the old lives always be easily resumed. And no few people wanted fresh starts and new departures.

In 1946 RKO General Pictures released the much-praised and highly successful motion picture *The Best Years of Our Lives*. Winning numerous Academy Awards and both popular and critical acclaim, the film since has seemed to capture the meaning of the war's aftermath—the "best years" that followed the "Good War." Yet as with Studs Terkel's oral history of wartime America, the title more than the content of the film has shaped understandings of the era. And like Terkel's book, the movie, which traced the return and readjustment of three veterans, often made its title seem sardonic. One of the veterans was a middle-aged banker; taken aback upon his return by the crassness of commercial life and the unsettling new autonomy of his children, he drank too much before reconciling himself to his life and career. Another was a young bombardier officer of working-class origins who returned to an unhappy wartime marriage and uncertain economic prospects; ultimately he left his wife, fell in love with the banker's daughter, and drew upon his wartime experience to begin a new life. The third was a sailor who lost both hands in the war; after considerable anxiety and tribulation, he married his next-door sweetheart and seemed ready for the difficulties that obviously lay ahead.

But though the film had the happy endings that Hollywood—and perhaps the postwar public—required, it was not so obvious that the three veterans in the film, or countless other Americans, were in fact enjoying the best years of their lives. The war had taken its toll, not only in the "butcher's bill" of the dead and wounded but in bruised psyches, disrupted lives, and home-front difficulties. Although wartime Americans ultimately realized more of their hopes than of their fears, and though they could later look back on the 1940s with warmth and nostalgia, neither the war years nor the early postwar era were quite as good or as happy as myth and memory later had it.

To be sure, World War II was an extraordinary time of triumphant common cause, a collective enterprise that vanquished the Axis and the Great Depression and launched a quarter-century of remarkable achievements and deserved

satisfactions. It contributed to a sense of American rectitude
and national power—and sometimes also to a belief that war
was the way to unity, prosperity, progress, and to solutions of
problems at home and abroad. For millions of Americans,
World War II was surely a Good War of national and personal accomplishment that lifted expectations as well as circumstances. For others, however, the war brought difficult
times or perpetuated old obstacles. For still others, the sense of
possibility at 1945 met frustration rather than fulfillment.

Whatever the varying outcomes for particular individuals
and groups, World War II had a large and lasting impact on
American life. The nation of V-J day and beyond was different from the one of Pearl Harbor and before. Most obviously,
World War II reshaped the global role of the United States
and made it the world's military, economic, and political powerhouse. But the war also changed the nation at home. Perhaps nothing so distinguished postwar from prewar America
as the expansive new realities and important consequences of
economic growth. Wartime mobilization had ended the depression, and production, employment, and income continued
to climb to unprecedented levels for years and decades after
the war. Together with the emphasis on family, rising expectations and living standards helped fuel the prodigious baby
boom of 1946 to 1964 with so many implications for postwar
American history.

Nor was that all. Wartime technological and scientific advances continued to shape important aspects of American life.
White ethnic groups continued to gain in economic standing,
social status, and political power. Many women over thirty-
five remained in the workforce while growing numbers of
young women pursued high school and college educations.
African Americans continued to organize and protest. The
populations of the suburbs and the Sunbelt swelled further.
The great postwar surge in religious affiliation accelerated the

wartime growth of church membership. The federal government was far larger, more expensive, and more powerful than it had been in the 1930s.

These and other wartime and postwar developments were not always welcomed. Many whites resisted black advances and black protest, for example, while women's changing roles stirred concern among people devoted to old ways and old norms. Divorce and juvenile delinquency loomed as larger problems than before and often seemed part of a general erosion of standards and behavior in a more prosperous and mobile society. The size and cost of government domestic programs concerned antistatist conservatives; the state's coercive and intrusive powers often worried liberals as well as conservatives. The continued rise of large institutions in the organizational society threatened and sometimes displaced small farmers and small businesses and raised concerns about "organization men" in "grey flannel suits" and the reign of large, faceless bureaucracies.

And much did not change. Old values and old norms remained powerful, not only with respect to race and gender but in many other areas of American life as well. Sharing traditional individualist values and middle-class aims, most people pursued the American dream of abundance, security, and the good life they had sought before and during the war. In many communities, life went on much as before. The United States remained an exceptionally religious nation. Long-term social and economic trends continued too, and much of the evident wartime and postwar change was only partly a result of the war. The nation was different after the war but not transformed; fundamental dynamics and patterns of life persisted.

Nor, finally, did politics, that important reflection of American life and culture, depart greatly from prewar and wartime patterns. Harry Truman won his stunning 1948 upset victory in an election where domestic issues predominated, economic security remained the major concern, and the core of the Democratic majority remained intact. In domestic policy too, basic continuity marked the 1940s and 1950s. Eroded at the margins and more vulnerable in a new context of affluence and global power, the Roosevelt coalition and the New Deal nonetheless remained the twin foci of the nation's politics and domestic policymaking far into the postwar era.

Yet the war left its mark on the political system, as it did on the nation. Although Democrats remained the majority party, Republicans had greater strength than before the war and politics were more conservative. The postwar liberal agenda—emphasizing full-employment prosperity and, increasingly, civil rights—differed from 1930s liberalism in significant ways. And World War II also had such diverse and sometimes diffuse effects on postwar politics as expanding the size and importance of the non-Southern black vote, contributing to the growing political influence of the Sunbelt states, weakening the Democrats' hold on the South, and propelling the GI generation to political activism and ultimately to national leadership.

Both change and continuity, often intertwined, characterized wartime America. Much that happened at home during the war was laudable and salutary, a good deal was lamentable, and some was deplorable. Rather than rendering a simple verdict on the watershed thesis or the idea of the Good War, one must see the war years in all their complexity and historical context. Only then can one discern the full nature and significance of the home-front experience and the complicated impact of World War II on the United States.

A Note on Sources

ALTHOUGH PRIMARILY a work of synthesis, this book also draws on my own research on the World War II home front. In that work I have consulted especially records in the Franklin D. Roosevelt Library, the National Archives, the Harry S. Truman Library, and the Roper Public Opinion Research Center; a variety of government publications; and a range of contemporary newspapers, magazines, and journals of opinion.

But *Wartime America* rests principally upon studies by other scholars. What follows is a brief listing of those I found most useful. Numerical data are taken from *The Statistical History of the United States from Colonial Times to the Present* (Stamford, Conn., 1965) as well as from the other sources listed; it should be noted that data on wartime America often vary, sometimes considerably, from source to source.

World War II was termed a "many-sided social revolution" by Eliot Janeway in *The Struggle for Survival: A Chronicle of Economic Mobilization in World War II* (New Haven, 1951), but the notion of a "watershed" began to inform modern historiography in the 1970s, especially after William H. Chafe's account of the impact of the war on women in *The American Woman: Her Changing Social, Economic, and Political Roles, 1920–1970* (New York, 1972), and Richard M. Dalfiume's *Desegregation of the U.S. Armed Forces: Fighting on Two Fronts, 1939–1953* (Columbia, Mo., 1969). In his excellent *War and Society: The United States, 1941–1945* (Philadelphia, 1972), Richard Polenberg maintained that Pearl Harbor "signified the end of an old era and the beginning of a new." Allan M. Winkler's *Home Front U.S.A.: America During World War II* (Arlington Heights, Ill., 1986), probes the watershed thesis and comes down more on the side of change

200 A NOTE ON SOURCES

than of continuity. John Morton Blum, *V Was for Victory: Politics and American Culture During World War II* (New York, 1976) is an illuminating study of wartime America emphasizing inertia and continuities. Kenneth Paul O'Brien and Lynn Hudson Parsons, eds., *The Home-Front War: World War II and American Society* (Westport, Conn., 1995) contains both a useful collection of essays and a detailed guide to recent studies of the home front. The *Washington Post* special section on World War II was published July 26, 1995.

A number of state and local studies have assessed the impact of World War II on American life. Those that emphasize change include Gerald D. Nash, *The American West Transformed: The Impact of the Second World War* (Bloomington, Ind., 1985); C. Calvin Smith, *War and Wartime Changes: The Transformation of Arkansas, 1940–1945* (Fayetteville, Ark., 1986); Morton Sosna, "More Important Than the Civil War? The Impact of World War II on the South," in *Perspectives on the American South*, 4 (1987), 145–161; and Pete Daniel, "Going Among Strangers: Southern Reactions to World War II," in *Journal of American History*, 77 (December 1990), 886–911. Local studies that in varying degrees find important continuities as well as change include Alan Clive, *State of War: Michigan in World War II* (Ann Arbor, 1979); John W. Jeffries, *Testing the Roosevelt Coalition: Connecticut Society and Politics in the Era of World War II* (Knoxville, 1979); Marc Scott Miller, *The Irony of Victory: World War II and Lowell, Massachusetts* (Urbana, Ill., 1988); and articles in the special issue of the *Pacific Historical Review*, 63 (August 1994), devoted to "Fortress California at War."

Paul Fussell's *Wartime: Understanding and Behavior in the Second World War* (New York, 1989) takes sharp issue with the notion of a "Good War," as does Richard Polenberg's "The Good War? A Reappraisal of How World War II Affected American Society," *Virginia Magazine of History and Biography*, 100 (July 1992), 295–322. Michael C. C. Adams, in his revisionist *The Best War Ever: America and World War II* (Baltimore, 1994), shows both sides of the war but seeks especially to counter popular notions of the Good War, while William L. O'Neill in *A Democracy at War: America's Fight at Home and Abroad in World War II* (New York, 1993) finds much to criticize but much also to celebrate. For the 1989 panel of American historians, see "A Round Table: The Living and Reliving of World War II," in the *Journal of American History*, 77 (September 1990), 553–593.

Important compilations of oral histories of the World War II home front include Studs Terkel, *"The Good War": An Oral History of World War II* (New York, 1984); Mark Jonathan Harris, Franklin Mitchell, and Steven Schechter, *The Homefront: America During World War II* (New York, 1984); Roy Hoopes, *Americans Remember the Homefront: An Oral Narrative* (New York, 1976); and Sherna B. Gluck, *Rosie the Riveter Revisited: Women, the War, and Social Change* (Boston, 1987).

Useful accounts of the impact of war on the state include Bruce D. Porter, *War and the Rise of the State: The Military Foundations of Modern Politics* (New York, 1994) and Arthur A. Stein, *The Nation at War* (Baltimore, 1980). John Kenneth Galbraith examines the postwar American economy in *American Capitalism: The Concept of Countervailing Power* (Boston, 1952, 1956). Bartholomew H. Sparrow makes a strong case for the impact of the war in *From the Outside In: World War II and the American State* (Princeton, 1996).

On Franklin D. Roosevelt and his wartime conduct of the presidency, see James MacGregor Burns, *Roosevelt: The Soldier of Freedom* (New York, 1970); Robert Dallek, *Franklin D. Roosevelt and American Foreign Policy, 1932–1945* (New York, 1981); Eric Larrabee, *Commander in Chief: Franklin Delano Roosevelt, His Lieutenants, and Their War* (New York, 1987); Warren F. Kimball, *The Juggler: Franklin Roosevelt as Wartime Statesman* (Princeton, 1991); Doris Kearns Goodwin, *No Ordinary Time: Franklin and Eleanor Roosevelt: The Home Front in World War II* (New York, 1994); and, John W. Jeffries, "Franklin D. Roosevelt and the 'America of Tomorrow,'" in David M. Kennedy and Michael E. Parrish, eds., *Power and Responsibility: Case Studies in American Leadership* (New York, 1986), pp. 29–66.

Harold G. Vatter provides an important analysis of the wartime economy and economic policy in *The U.S. Economy in World War II* (New York, 1985). Alan S. Milward, *War, Economy and Society: 1939–1945* (Berkeley, 1977); Peter Fearon, *War, Prosperity and Depression: The U.S. Economy 1917–45* (Oxford, England, 1987); and, James L. Abrahamson, *The American Home Front* (Washington, D.C., 1983) provide useful data and perspectives. Robert Higgs challenges the notion of wartime prosperity in "Wartime Prosperity? A Reassessment of the U.S. Economy in the 1940s," *Journal of Economic History*, 52 (March 1992), 41–60.

On economic mobilization, Janeway, cited above, remains useful. Gerald D. Nash explores the war's impact on the "organizational society" in *The Crucial Era: The Great Depression and World War II, 1929–1945*, 2nd ed. (New York, 1992). On big business and the military, see Bruce Catton, *The War Lords of Washington* (New York, 1948); Paul A. C. Koistinen, *The Military Industrial Complex: A Historical Perspective* (New York, 1980); Gregory Hooks, *Forging the Military-Industrial Complex: World War II's Battle of the Potomac* (Urbana, Ill., 1991); and Jonathan J. Bean, "World War II and the 'Crisis' of Small Business: The Smaller War Plants Corporation, 1942–1946, *Journal of Policy History*, 6 (1994), 215–243. On labor and management, see Nelson Lichtenstein, *Labor's War at Home: The CIO in World War II* (New York, 1982) and Howell John Harris, *The Right to Manage: Industrial Relations Policies of American Business in the 1940s* (Madison, Wisc., 1982). See also Nicholas Lemann, Introduction to "In the Forties," *Atlantic Monthly*, January 1983, 39–43.

On Keynesianism and fiscal policy, see Herbert Stein, *The Fiscal Revolution in America* (Chicago, 1969). For the redirection of American liberalism, see Alan Brinkley, *The End of Reform: New Deal Liberalism in Recession and War* (New York, 1995); John W. Jeffries, "The 'New' New Deal: FDR and American Liberalism, 1937–1945," *Political Science Quarterly* (Fall 1990), 397–418; and Jeffries, "A 'Third New Deal'? Liberal Policy and the American State, 1937–1945," *Journal of Policy History*, 8:4 (1996).

Philip Funigiello examines wartime migration and urban policy in *The Challenge to Urban Liberalism: Federal-City Relations During World War II* (Knoxville, 1978). In addition to works by Nash, Sosna, and Daniel on the West and South, see David R. Goldfield, *Promised Land: The South Since 1945* (Arlington Heights, Ill., 1987) and Numan V. Bartley, *The New South, 1945–1980* (Baton Rouge, 1995). Many of the books cited elsewhere discuss wartime community change and stress, but see also David Brinkley, *Washington Goes to War* (New York, 1988).

William M. Tuttle, Jr., provides an illuminating, multifaceted study of wartime families and children in *"Daddy's Gone to War": The Second World War in the Lives of America's Children* (New York, 1993). *Since You Went Away: World War II Letters from American Women on the Home Front* (New York, 1991), ed. by Judy Barrett Litoff and David C. Smith, is useful on wartime families, as are relevant parts of Susan M. Hartmann, *The Home Front and Beyond: American Women in the 1940s* (Boston, 1982) and D'Ann Campbell, *Women at War with America: Private Lives in a Patriotic Era* (Cambridge, Mass., 1984). See also John Costello, *Virtue Under Fire: How World War II Changed Our Social and Sexual Attitudes* (Boston, 1985) and Beth Bailey and David Farber, *The First Strange Place: The Alchemy of Race and Sex in World War II Hawaii* (New York, 1992).

The literature on World War II and American women has become extraordinarily prolific and sophisticated. I relied especially on the books by Hartmann, Campbell, Chafe, and Gluck cited earlier as well as on Karen Anderson, *Wartime Women: Sex Roles, Family Relations, and the Status of Women During World War II* (Westport, Conn., 1983); Claudia Goldin, *Understanding the Gender Gap: An Economic History of American Women* (New York, 1990); and Goldin, "The Role of World War II in the Rise of Women's Employment," *American Economic Review*, 81 (September 1991), 741–756. Chafe's book has been revised and reissued as *The Paradox of Change: American Women in the 20th Century* (New York, 1991). Other significant studies include Mary Martha Thomas, *Riveting and Rationing in Dixie: Alabama Women and the Second World War* (Tuscaloosa, Ala., 1987); Amy

Kesselman, *Fleeting Opportunities: Women Shipyard Workers in Portland and Vancouver During World War II and Reconversion* (Albany, 1990); Ruth Milkman, *Gender at Work: The Dynamics of Job Segregation by Sex During World War II* (Urbana, Ill., 1987); and Leila J. Rupp, *Mobilizing Women for War: German and American Propaganda, 1939–1945* (Princeton, 1978).

For World War II and black Americans, the best general account remains Neil A. Wynn, *The Afro-American and the Second World War*, rev. ed. (New York, 1993). In a substantial literature, see also the study by Dalfiume cited earlier; Merl E. Reed, *Seedtime for the Modern Civil Rights Movement: The President's Committee on Fair Employment Practice, 1941–1946* (Baton Rouge, 1991); Louis Ruchames, *Race, Jobs, and Politics: The Story of FEPC* (Chapel Hill, 1948); John B. Kirby, *Black Americans in the Roosevelt Era: Liberalism and Race* (Knoxville, 1980); Lee Finkle, *Forum for Protest: The Black Press During World War II* (Rutherford, N.J., 1975); Leonard Broom and Norval D. Glenn, *Transformation of the Negro American* (New York, 1965); Patrick S. Washburn, *A Question of Sedition: The Federal Government's Investigation of the Black Press During World War II* (New York, 1986); Dominic J. Capeci, *The Harlem Riot of 1943* (Philadelphia, 1977); John Modell, et al., "World War II in the Lives of Black Americans: Some Findings and an Interpretation," *Journal of American History*, 76 (December 1989), 838–848; Norval D. Glenn, "Some Changes in the Relative Status of American Nonwhites, 1940–1960," *Phylon*, 24 (Summer 1963), 109–122; Harvard Sitkoff, "Racial Militancy and Interracial Violence in the Second World War," *Journal of American History*, 58 (December 1971), 661–681; and Peter J. Kellogg, "Civil Rights Consciousness in the 1940s," *The Historian*, 42 (November 1979), 18–41.

Aspects of wartime ethnic history are addressed in Philip Gleason, "Americans All: World War II and the Shaping of American Identity," *Review of Politics*, 43 (October 1981), 483–518; Richard Polenberg, *One Nation Divisible: Class, Race, and Ethnicity in the United States Since 1938* (New York, 1980); and Richard W. Steele, "'No Racials': Discrimination Against

Ethnics in American Defense Industry, 1940–42," *Labor History*,
32 (Winter 1991), 66–90. Stephen Fox, *The Unknown Internment:
An Oral History of the Relocation of Italian Americans During
World War II* (Boston, 1990) and George E. Pozzetta, "'My Chil-
dren Are My Jewels': Italian-American Generations During
World War II," pp. 63–82 in O'Brien and Parsons cited earlier,
examine the experiences of Italian Americans, while in a larger
literature Audrie Girdner and Anne Loftis, *The Great Betrayal:
The Evacuation of the Japanese-Americans During World War II*
(New York, 1969); Roger Daniels, *Concentration Camps U.S.A.:
Japanese Americans and World War II* (New York, 1971); Daniels,
The Decision to Relocate the Japanese Americans (Philadelphia,
1975); Daniels, *Prisoners Without Trial: Japanese Americans in
World War II* (New York, 1993); Peter Irons, *Justice at War* (New
York, 1983); and Page Smith, *Democracy on Trial: The Japanese
American Evacuation and Relocation in World War II* (New York,
1995) are good on the relocation of Japanese Americans. On anti-
Semitism and American policy, see David S. Wyman, *The Aban-
donment of the Jews: America and the Holocaust, 1941–1945* (New
York, 1984). Alison R. Bernstein, *American Indians and World
War II* (Norman, Okla., 1991) is now the standard study on its
subject, as is Allan Bérubé, *Coming Out Under Fire: The History of
Gay Men and Women in World War II* (New York, 1990).

On politics, see in addition to books by Blum, Jeffries, and
Polenberg cited earlier, Herbert S. Parmet and Marie B. Hecht,
Never Again: A President Runs for a Third Term (New York, 1968);
Samuel Lubell, *The Future of American Politics* 3rd rev. ed. (New
York, 1965); Everett C. Ladd, Jr., with Charles D. Hadley, *Trans-
formations of the American Party System: Political Coalitions from
the New Deal to the 1970s*, 2nd rev. ed. (New York, 1978); V. O.
Key, Jr., *The Responsible Electorate: Rationality in Presidential Vot-
ing, 1936–1960* (Cambridge, Mass., 1966); Paul F. Lazarsfeld, et
al., *The People's Choice*, 3rd ed. (New York, 1968); Robert A. Di-
vine, *Foreign Policy and U.S. Presidential Elections, 1940–1948*
(New York, 1974); and Robert E. Burke, "Election of 1940," and
Leon Friedman, "Election of 1944," both in Arthur M.

206 A NOTE ON SOURCES

Schlesinger, ed., *History of American Presidential Elections, 1789–1968*, vol. IV (New York, 1971), 2917–3006 and 3009–3096.

For wartime policymaking, see in addition to studies cited earlier, Richard N. Chapman, *Contours of Public Policy, 1939–1945* (New York, 1981); Roland Young, *Congressional Politics in the Second World War* (New York, 1956); David Brody, "The New Deal and World War II," in John Braeman, et al., eds., *The New Deal*, I (Columbus, Ohio, 1975), pp. 267–309; Edwin Amenta and Theda Skocpol, "Redefining the New Deal: World War II and the Development of Social Provision in the United States," in Margaret Weir, et al., *The Politics of Social Policy in the United States* (Princeton, 1988), pp. 81–122; Philip Warken, *A History of the National Resources Planning Board, 1933–1943* (New York, 1979); and Stephen Kemp Bailey, *Congress Makes a Law: The Story Behind the Employment Act of 1946* (New York, 1950).

A huge literature on the World War II armed forces is nicely summarized in D. Clayton James and Anne Sharp Wells, *From Pearl Harbor to V-J Day: The American Armed Forces in World War II* (Chicago, 1995); Lee Kennett, *G.I.: The American Soldier in World War II* (New York, 1987); and John Ellis, *The Sharp End: The Fighting Man in World War II* (New York, 1980). Samuel A. Stouffer, *The American Soldier*, 2 vols. (Princeton, 1949) provides an indispensable compendium of GI opinion. On the GI Bill, see Davis R. B. Ross, *Preparing for Ulysses: Politics and Veterans During World War II* (New York, 1969) and Keith Olson, *The G.I. Bill, the Veterans, and the Colleges* (Lexington, Ky., 1974).

On home-front life, in addition to other studies cited, Richard R. Lingeman, *Don't You Know There's a War On: The American Home Front, 1941–1945* (New York, 1970) and Geoffrey Perrett, *Days of Sadness, Years of Triumph: The American People, 1939–1945* (New York, 1973) provide lively and informative accounts. Among contemporary studies of the home front, Selden Menefee, *Assignment: USA* (New York, 1943); Agnes E. Meyer, *Journey Through Chaos* (New York, 1944); John Dos Passos, *State of the Nation* (Boston, 1944); Jack Goodman, ed., *While You Were Gone: A Report on Wartime Life in the United States* (New York,

1946); and Francis E. Merrill, *Social Problems on the Home Front: A Study of War-time Influences* (New York, 1948) stand out.

For efforts to shape views of the war, see Allan M. Winkler, *The Politics of Propaganda: The Office of War Information, 1942–1945* (New Haven, 1978); Clayton R. Koppes and Gregory D. Black, *Hollywood Goes to War: How Politics, Profits, and Propaganda Shaped World War II Movies* (New York, 1987); Thomas Doherty, *Projections of War: Hollywood, American Culture, and World War II* (New York, 1993); and, George H. Roeder, Jr., *The Censored War: American Visual Experience During World War Two* (New Haven, 1993). Frank W. Fox, *Madison Avenue Goes to War: The Strange Military Career of American Advertising, 1941–45* (Provo, Utah, 1975), examines wartime advertising.

Jerome S. Bruner, *Mandate from the People* (New York, 1944) is a penetrating analysis of wartime public opinion. Hadley Cantril, ed. *Public Opinion, 1935–1946* (Princeton, 1951) is an invaluable compendium of opinion surveys.

For varying portraits and assessments of early postwar America, see, in an abundant literature, Eric F. Goldman, *The Crucial Decade—And After: America, 1945–1960* (New York, 1960); Howard Zinn, *Postwar America, 1945–1971* (Indianapolis, 1973); Joseph C. Goulden, *The Best Years, 1945–1950* (New York, 1976); William L. O'Neill, *American High: The Years of Confidence, 1945–1960* (New York, 1986); John P. Diggins, *The Proud Decades: America in War and Peace, 1941–1960* (New York, 1988); and James T. Patterson, *Grand Expectations: The United States, 1945–1974* (New York, 1996).

Index

A NOTE ON THE AUTHOR

John W. Jeffries is professor of history and chair of the department at the University of Maryland Baltimore County. Born in Oxford, Mississippi, he grew up in Annapolis, Maryland, and later received his B.A. from Harvard and his Ph.D. from Yale. He has written frequently on the politics and policies of the Franklin D. Roosevelt administration, and is the author of *Testing the Roosevelt Coalition* and co-author of *While Soldiers Fought: War and American Society.*

BOOKS IN THE AMERICAN WAYS SERIES

William Earl Weeks, *Building the Continental Empire: American Expansion from the Revolution to the Civil War*

Jean V. Matthews, *Women's Struggle for Equality: The First Phase, 1820–1876*

Curtis D. Johnson, *Redeeming America: Evangelicals and the Road to Civil War*

J. Matthew Gallman, *The North Fights the Civil War: The Home Front*

Maury Klein, *The Flowering of the Third America: The Making of an Organizational Society, 1850–1920*

Larry M. Logue, *To Appomattox and Beyond: The Civil War Soldier in War and Peace*

Robert Muccigrosso, *Celebrating the New World: Chicago's Columbian Exposition of 1893*

Daniel Nelson, *Shifting Fortunes: The Rise and Decline of American Labor, from the 1820s to the Present*

Thomas R. Pegram, *Battling Demon Rum: The Struggle for a Dry America, 1800–1933*

Roger Daniels, *Not Like Us: Immigrants and Minorities in America, 1890–1924*

Burton W. Peretti, *Jazz in American Culture*

Iwan W. Morgan, *Deficit Government: Taxing and Spending in Modern America*

D. Clayton James and Anne Sharp Wells, *From Pearl Harbor to V-J Day: The American Armed Forces in World War II*

John W. Jeffries, *Wartime America: The World War II Home Front*

John Earl Haynes, *Red Scare or Red Menace?: American Communism and Anticommunism in the Cold War Era*

Mark J. White, *Missiles in Cuba: Kennedy, Khrushchev, Castro, and the 1962 Crisis*

John A. Salmond, *"My Mind Set on Freedom": A History of the Civil Rights Movement, 1954–1968*

John A. Andrew III, *Lyndon Johnson and the Great Society*

Kenneth J. Heineman, *Put Your Bodies upon the Wheels: Student Revolt in the 1960s*

Lewis L. Gould, *1968: The Election That Changed America*

Hal K. Rothman, *Saving the Planet: The American Response to the Environment in the Twentieth Century*

Kevin White, *Sexual Liberation or Sexual License?: The American Revolt Against Victorianism*

Made in the USA
San Bernardino, CA
06 June 2016